Artur Landt/Bob Shell

Canon EOS-3

Magic Lantern Guides

Canon EOS-3

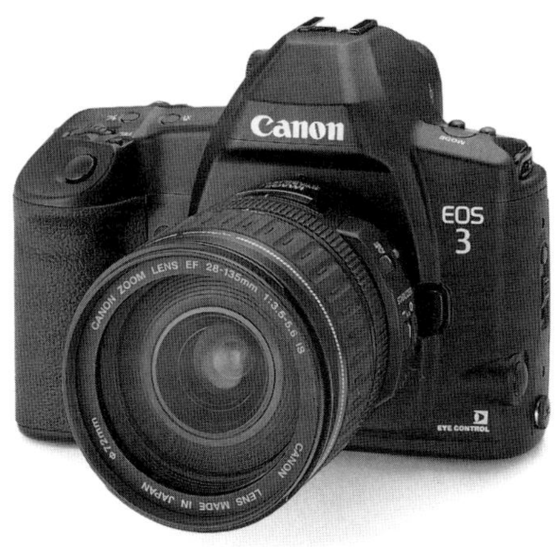

Artur Landt/Bob Shell

Magic Lantern Guide to
Canon EOS-3

Second Printing 2000
Published in the United States of America by

Silver Pixel Press®
A Tiffen® Company
21 Jet View Drive
Rochester, NY 14624
Fax: (716) 328-5078
www.silverpixelpress.com

ISBN 1-883403-59-6

From the German edition by Artur Landt
Translated and edited by Bob Shell
Text on pages 124-168 taken from the *Magic Lantern Guide to Canon EOS Rebel 2000,* courtesy of Heiner Henninges.
Printed in Germany by Kösel GmbH, Kempten

Library of Congress Cataloging-in-Publication Data
Shell, Bob.
Canon EOS-3 / Bob Shell, Artur Landt.
p. cm. — (Magic lantern guides)
ISBN 1-883403-59-6 (pbk.)
1. Canon camera—Handbooks, manuals, etc. 2. Single-lens-reflex cameras—Handbooks, manuals, etc. I. Landt, Artur, 1958- . II. Title. III. Series.
TR263,C3 S543 2000
77.3′2—dc21 00-023928

Contents

EOS Controls

The Canon EOS-3—a single-lens-reflex (SLR) camera, in which the image produced by the lens is reflected by a mirror to the viewfinder and corresponds accurately to the image field—has been conceived and designed for professional use. Familiarizing yourself with the names and locations of the controls before going further will help make the reading and use of the rest of this book easier. All specifications refer to the camera in horizontal position; the terms "left" and "right" refer to the camera in the shooting position.

The most important control elements of the EOS-3 are the Main Dial (behind the shutter release) and the Quick Control Dial (on the camera back); the Quick Control Dial is turned on and off by the switch above it. Both controls have a variety of functions depending upon how the camera is set up for use by the individual photographer.

Three function selector buttons are on the upper left side of the EOS-3 camera body: the shooting mode selector (marked "MODE"), the AF mode button (marked "AF"), and the exposure compensation button. After pressing these function buttons, individually or in sets of two, you can make the appropriate selections and adjustments with the Main Dial and the Quick Control Dial.

Select the exposure Program by pressing the shooting mode selector, and scroll with the Main Dial until the desired mode (P, Av, Tv, M, DEP, buLb) is displayed on the LCD panel on top of the camera. Pressing the shooting mode selector and scrolling the Main Dial selects the AF operating mode (One Shot or AI Servo) as well. If the AF mode button and the shooting mode selector are pressed at the same time, autoexposure bracketing can be engaged, and the Main Dial can be used to set the amount of bracketing around the camera's determined exposure.

The exposure compensation button is used for several purposes: by pressing the button and turning the Main Dial, you can select the exposure metering type (evaluative, partial, spot, multi-spot, center-weighted average), while the Quick Control Dial sets

Canon EOS-3—Top

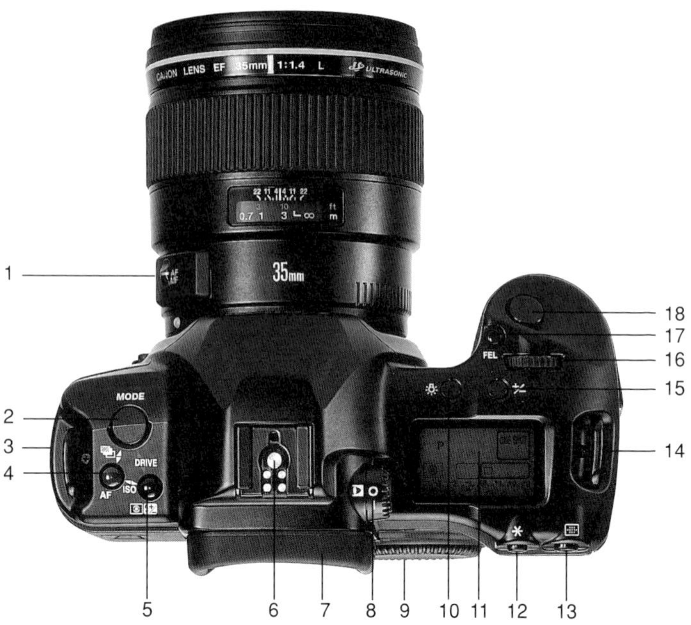

1. AF/MF switch
2. Shooting mode selector (Mode button)
3. Strap eyelet
4. AF mode button
5. Exposure compensation button
6. X-sync contact
7. Hot shoe
8. Eye-control switch
9. Quick control dial
10. LCD panel illumination button
11. LCD panel
12. AE lock button
13. Focusing point selector
14. Strap eyelet
15. Exposure compensation/ Aperture button
16. Main dial
17. Flash exposure lock (FEL)/ Multispot metering button
18. Shutter release button

the exposure correction. If the exposure compensation and the AF mode buttons are pressed at the same time, the exposure index can be changed manually with the Main Dial. If the exposure compensation button and the shooting mode selector are pressed at the same time, the film advance (single or series) and the self-timer (two or ten seconds) can be set with the Main Dial.

Canon EOS-3—Front

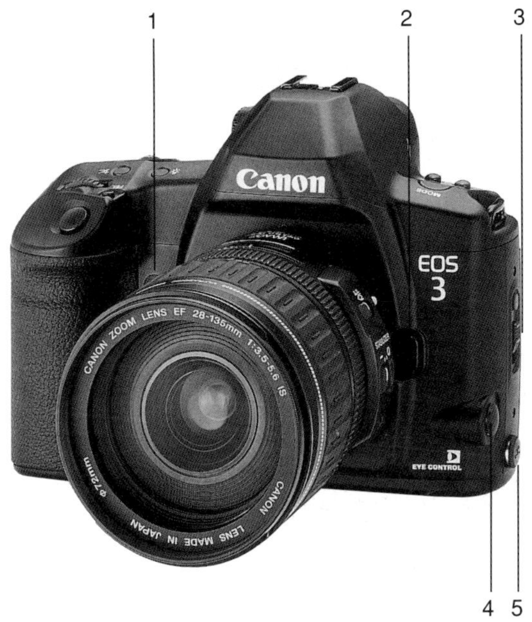

1. Self-timer lamp
2. Lens release button
3. Camera back release
4. Remote control socket
5. PC terminal

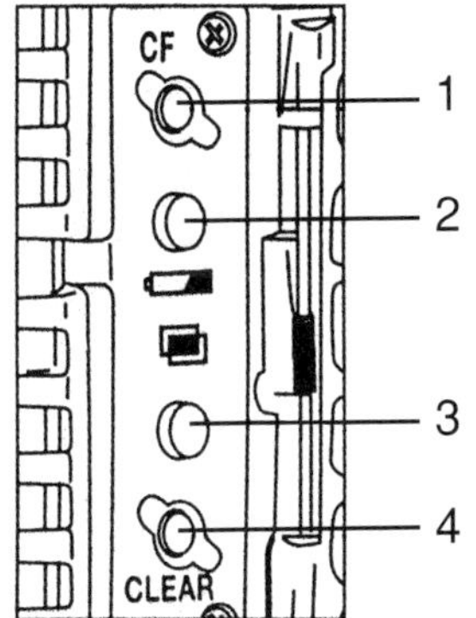

Spring Door Controls

1. Custom Function setting
2. Battery check
3. Multiple exposure button
4. Clear

Canon EOS-3—Back

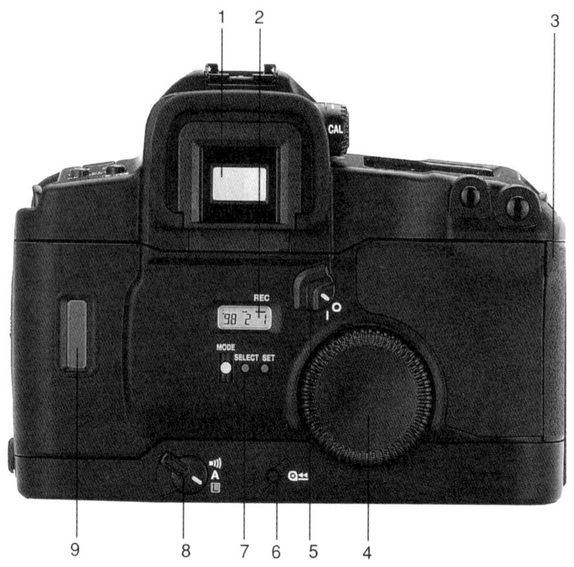

1. **Viewfinder**
2. **Date back**
3. **Side door**
4. **Quick control dial**
5. **Quick control dial on/off switch**
6. **Midroll rewind button**
7. **Date back control buttons**
8. **Main switch**
9. **Film window**

The main switch, on the back of the camera, switches the camera from A (on) to L (lock) and activates the beeper (if desired) as focus confirmation. The button for midroll rewinding (for rewinding partially exposed rolls of film) is located on the right beside the main switch.

Below the right upper camera edge are two small buttons. The left one, the AE lock button, marked with an *, is used to record exposure information into memory; the one on the right, the focusing point selector, lets you choose the AF sensor area. On the right end of the camera is a spring door, under which are controls for functions less often used; here you will find the Custom Functions button, the battery check button, the multiple exposure setting button, and the Clear button, for resetting the factory default camera settings.

Canon EOS-3—Bottom

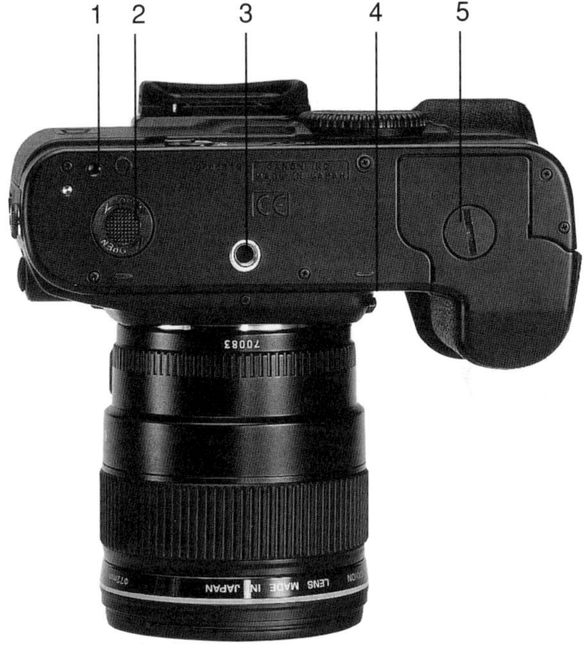

1. **Pin registration hole for power drive booster**
2. **Film transport coupling for power drive booster**
3. **Tripod socket**
4. **Depth-of-field preview button**
5. **Battery compartment**

In the view of the bottom side, the manual stopdown button is located between the handgrip and the lens bayonet mount. Pressing this button closes the lens diaphragm to its set value so that a visual check of the depth of field is possible. The battery compartment is in the handgrip and is accessible from the bottom. To open it, use a coin to unscrew the cover. The PB-E2 power drive booster can be attached in place of the battery compartment cover. The switch for turning the eye-control autofocus on and off and for calibration of the eye control is located on the prism housing (to the right of the hot shoe).

The Flash Exposure Lock (FEL)/multispot metering, the LCD illuminator, and the manual exposure correction/aperture setting (+/–) buttons are on the upper right side of the EOS-3.

Testing Your Camera

Testing the EOS-3—activating and deactivating the individual camera functions without using film—increases the camera's electrical consumption in the beginning, but the practice you do will help you be more efficient with film in the long run. Therefore, we recommend practice—particularly with as richly equipped a camera as the Canon EOS-3; for example, place the AF measuring fields on a wide variety of subjects to become familiar with the system's function.

It won't be long before you are producing great pictures with your EOS-3!

Before Using the EOS-3

The Canon EOS-3 is a complex, computerized photographic instrument, incorporating many features that can be adjusted to suit the preferences and habits of the individual photographer—adding eyesight correction lenses to the viewfinder or calibrating the eye control to the photographer's eye, for example.

It is definitely exciting to photograph with the new Canon EOS-3 for the first time. Because of its brilliant technology, this camera has a special fascination. The first-time user will most likely want a little guidance and reassurance, however; that is why we begin with a chapter on the basics in a guide to a professional camera like the EOS-3—because it will be bought not only by professionals, but also by many amateurs who seek to become professional or semi-professional in their photography. We recommend that you review the chapter completely before coming back to it with your camera and following our instructions for operation.

Attaching the Neck Strap

The neck strap that came with your EOS-3 has an important protective function. It can save your camera from a fall to the ground or—what is much worse—a fall onto hard pavement; it also makes carrying the camera, as well as lens and film changing, simpler and more secure. For these reasons, you should attach the neck strap as your first action after unpacking the camera.

After unpacking the strap, make sure that each of its end sections is pulled out from the retaining loop and buckle. It doesn't matter which side of the camera you attach the strap to first; we will describe starting on the left. Slip the end of the strap through the slotted strap lug from the outside in and pull several inches through the slot. Now draw up the strap portion that is passing through the black plastic buckle, and slide the loose end of the strap first through the retaining loop and then push the end of it up inside the buckle from below so that it passes from the lower buckle slot upward into the loop you made. Bend the end of it over inside the loop of strap and pass it back down through the other slot in the buckle. Then, pull the strap taut.

Whatever side you started on, you must now repeat the process in mirror image on the other side. Check the length; if it is too long, loosen the buckles and draw more of the strap through on the inner side until the length pleases you. What length is right? It is purely a matter of personal preference. There is no right and wrong in strap lengths.

You may think that such a strap can't possibly hold its place in the buckle without some sort of prong and hole as there is on your belt buckle, but it will stay in place just fine. The authors have used straps like this for years and have never experienced one coming loose accidentally.

Changing the Lens

Most photographers who buy the EOS-3 will most likely have more than one lens to use on their camera. The procedure for removing and attaching a lens is simple: When you first unpack the camera, there will be a black protective plastic body cap on the lens mount; to mount a lens, grasp the cap and turn it counterclockwise until it comes loose. Put the cap in a safe place for future use, such as when you want to store the camera body and lens separately in a camera bag to conserve space. Canon EF lenses are also provided with protective caps on the back, and these are removed the same way.

Once the lens and camera caps are out of the way, you can mount the lens. Simply line up the red dot on the lens barrel with the red dot at the top of the camera body bayonet, slip the lens into the bayonet until it is seated, and turn it clockwise until it

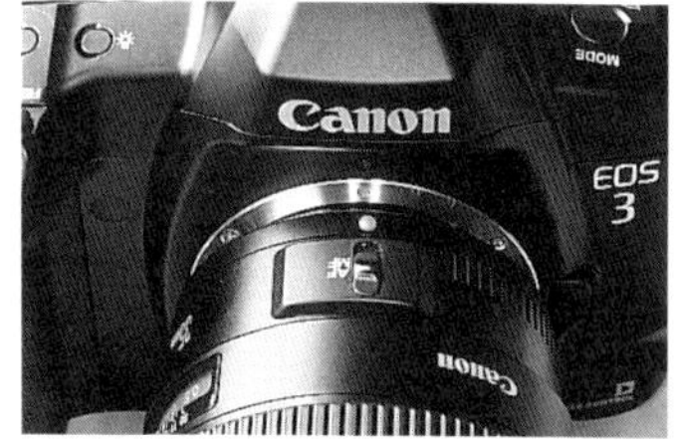

When attaching or removing EF lenses, make sure that the raised red dot on the lens barrel lines up with the red mark on the top of the camera body's bayonet mount. Once the lens is on the camera, turn it clockwise until it clicks into place.

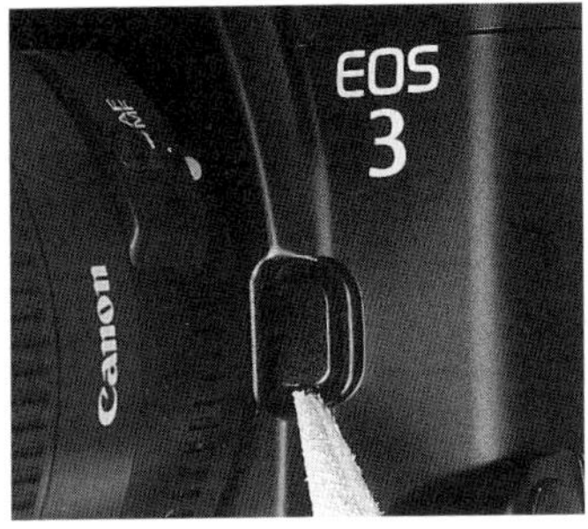

The lens release button is shown here just to the right of the lens mounting bayonet.

clicks into place. Check that it is secure by trying to give it a gentle turn back counterclockwise; if it is fully seated and locked, it will not turn. To remove a lens, press in on the lens release button (to the right of the lens when viewed from the front), and then turn the lens counterclockwise until it is free.

Because Canon EF lenses operate by electrical contacts with the camera body, it is best to switch the camera off before changing lenses. (Your authors confess, however, that in the hurry of real-life photography they generally forget to do this and have never had a camera harmed by this.) We also recommend changing lenses in the shade, if possible, when working outdoors—even just using the shade of your body when nothing else is handy. Always make sure your camera's neck strap is around your neck when changing lenses.

Lens Carrying Bags

Lens carrying bags are good protection against sand, dirt, and rain, and the best ones also keep out fine dust. Give serious consideration to the type of bag you buy to protect your new camera and its lenses. There are lots of brands and types of photo bags on the market, and your choice will ultimately come down to personal preference. Many professional photographers have depended on Domke® photo bags for years. They perform all of the necessary tasks admirably and can be highly recommended. Those photographers more interested in high style may want to take a look at the photo bags from Kipling.

Batteries

The Canon EOS-3 uses the readily available 2CR5 lithium battery as its power source. Before installing the battery, make sure that the contacts on the battery and in the camera are clean and free of grease by wiping them well with a soft, lint-free cotton cloth; a man's handkerchief is ideal. This ensures optimal contact and free flow of electricity. If there is stubborn material that will not come off the contacts, gentle rubbing with a pencil eraser is recommended. Be sure to blow away gently any residue from the eraser.

To open the battery container, turn the cover-retaining screw counterclockwise with a coin until the cover comes free and slips off in a downward direction; turn the gray battery retainer out of the way. Insert the 2CR5 lithium battery into the battery compartment, with the contacts downward and to the inside. The polarity (+/–) is indicated inside the battery compartment. The battery compartment should now be turned counterclockwise until it rests in the handgrip. Replace the camera handgrip and firmly tighten the retaining screw with a coin.

Although the camera automatically shuts off its displays when not used for a while, this does not turn it fully off; accidental pressure on the shutter release button can trip the camera and waste film. When putting the camera away, make it a point to always turn the main switch on the camera back to the L position. This will give you maximum possible battery life. To check the battery condition at any time, pull open the hinged door on the right end of the camera and press the small button marked with a picture of a battery. When you do this, you will see an

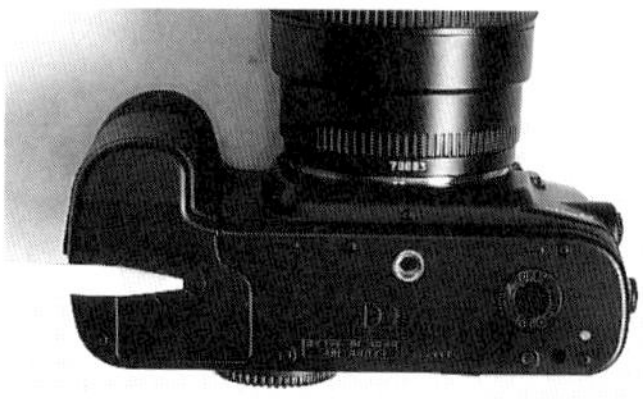

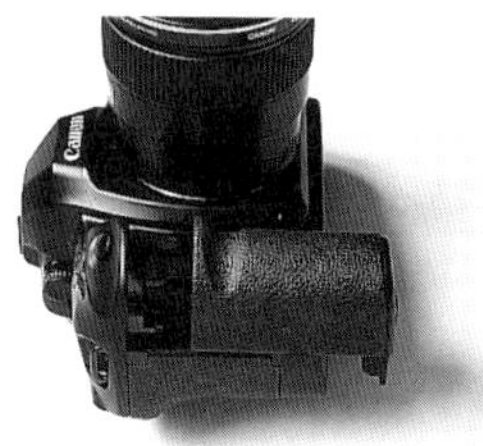

Remove the battery compartment cover by loosening the retaining screw with a coin; after the screw is loosened, the battery compartment cover slides downward to come off.

indication at the bottom of the camera's LCD panel indicating battery condition. The indication is in the form of dashes: three dashes (- - -) indicates that the battery condition is good, with a full or almost full charge; two dashes (- -) indicates that the battery condition is beginning to fade, so have a replacement battery ready; a flashing single dash (-) means that the battery is almost dead and should be replaced immediately, even though a few more photographs might be possible; a flashing "bc" (battery check) means that the battery power is nearly gone and that the camera will cease to function until a new battery is installed.

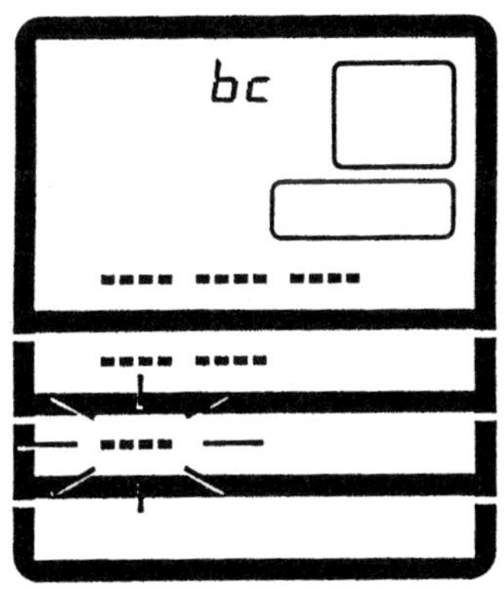

This diagram shows the four levels of battery power indicated when the battery test button is pressed.

If you get the flashing bc signal with a battery that you think should be good, take the battery out and clean it and the contacts in the camera thoroughly, and install it again. If you still get a flashing bc signal, the battery is defective or the camera is in need of factory service. To determine which, install a new battery you are sure is good and try again.

Sometimes it is possible to squeeze a few more photos out of a dying battery if you allow it to recover by switching the camera off for a few minutes. This is recommended only for an emergency situation, however, and not as something to resort to every time a battery becomes low.

Battery Condition

Lithium batteries are used in almost all current cameras because they have excellent characteristics as power sources for cameras.

They can handle high maximum load, operate over a very wide range of temperatures, have a very flat discharge curve over their lifespan, and can be stored up to ten years prior to use. With prolonged storage, however, these batteries sometimes "fall asleep." If this happens, they can usually be brought back to life by activating the camera without film several times in rapid succession. Even better, get a roll of outdated film and reserve it for tests and occasions like this by using it over and over.

Viewfinder

On a modern computerized camera like the EOS-3, the information display in the viewfinder has a particularly significant role. On the focusing screen, you will first notice the elliptical area marked off with a thin line; this shows the boundaries of the AF system. The 45 AF sensors are arranged in a pattern inside this ellipse. During AF operation, the active sensors are indicated by lighting up red. The small central circle, 0.2 inch (5 mm) in diameter, indicates the measuring area of the spot meter. Of course, if you wish, you can turn off the autofocus with the switch on the lens and manually focus by observing the sharpness and subject contrast on the viewing screen; with autofocus this good, however, we can imagine few occasions when anyone would want to do this. If you do choose to use manual focus, you can also confirm it by observing the round yellow-green dot focus indicator display under the image area in the viewfinder.

LCD Panel

The full-information LCD panel on top of the camera is the main indicator of the camera functions. It informs you of all settings as you use the camera and make any changes. In the accompanying diagram, all possible parts of the display are shown, but it will not look like this in use because only the active features will be displayed. To enable you to read the LCD panel in dim light, it is equipped with an illuminator, which can be turned on by the button just above it; the button shows an icon of a light bulb. To conserve battery power, the illuminator automatically switches off

Canon EOS-3—Viewfinder

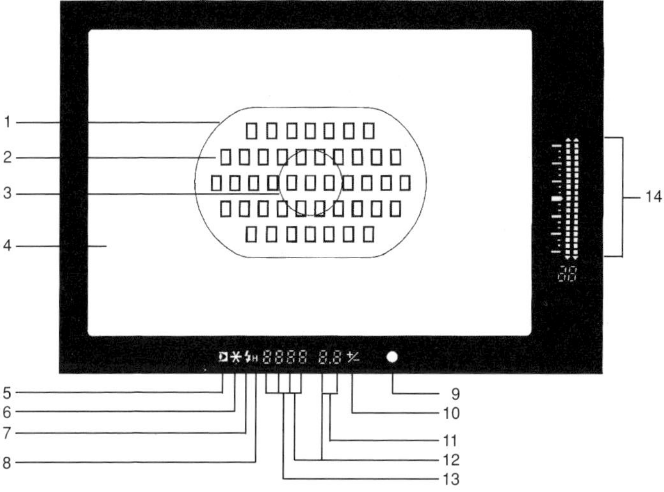

1. **Area AF ellipse**
2. **Focusing points (lights at the required point)**
3. **Center spot metering circle**
4. **Laser matte screen**
5. **Eye-control AF icon**
6. **AE lock indicator**
7. **Flash-ready/Flash exposure lock (FEL) warning indicator**
8. **High-speed-sync (FP) flash indicator**
9. **In-focus indicator**
10. **Exposure compensation/Flash exposure compensation icon**
11. **Aperture/Autofocus/ Calibration step display**
12. **Calibration/DEP/Focusing point selection mode display**
13. **FEL display/Shutter speed display**
14. **Three exposure indicators (vertical, left to right):**
    - **Exposure-level scale**
    - **Overexposure indicator**
    - **Flash overexposure indicator**

after about eight seconds. It can be manually switched off by pressing the button again.

Like all LCD displays, at very hot temperatures this one will cease to function and display all black. At very cold temperatures, around freezing, the LCD may slow down greatly. Both of these conditions are temporary, and the LCD will return to normal functioning after being in more comfortable temperatures for a short time. Neither of these conditions will prevent the camera from functioning, however, and if you cannot see the settings you

Canon EOS-3—LCD Panel

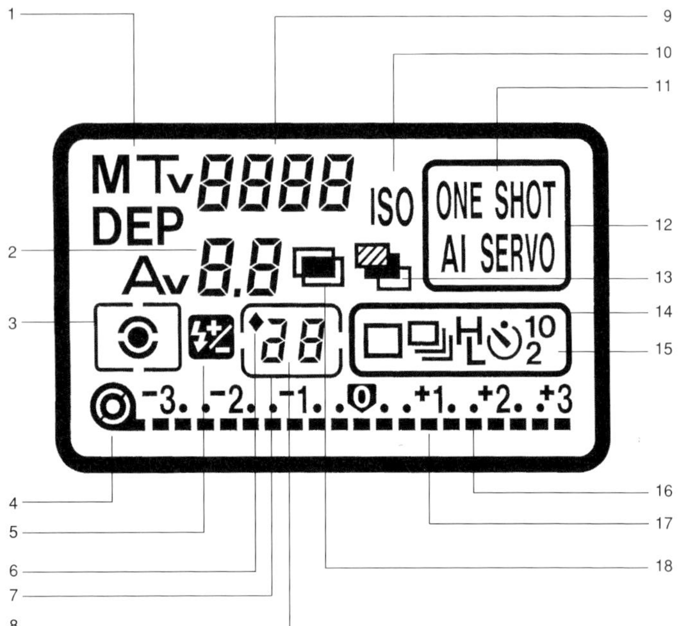

1. Exposure mode
2. Autoexposure bracketing (AEB) amount/Aperture/Calibration channel/Custom Function setting/Focusing point selection mode display
3. Metering mode
4. Film-loaded/Film rewind indicator
5. Flash exposure compensation
6. Remaining frame indicator
7. Frame counter box
8. Bulb exposure timer/Frame counter/Multiple exposure setting/Multiple exposures remaining/Self-timer countdown
9. Battery check/Calibration display/Custom Function/DEP AE point/Film speed/Flash exposure lock (FEL) button/Focusing point selection mode/Shutter speed display
10. ISO icon
11. AF mode
12. AF mode display box
13. AEB icon
14. Film transport display box
15. Film transport modes (left to right): single-frame shooting, continuous shooting (high and low speed), self-timer
16. Exposure compensation scale
17. AEB/Exposure compensation amount/Battery check/Bulb exposure timer/Custom Function setting/Film transport operation
18. Multiple exposure icon

may want to use just the autoexposure modes and trust the camera to do its job.

Over the years, the LCD panel may fade and darken. Should this happen (but one of the authors has Canon cameras over fifteen years old with LCD panels that have shown no fading), you may have the LCD replaced at a Canon service center.

Eyesight Correction

Even with an AF camera, a clear and sharp viewfinder is important for composition of the pictures, for visual verification of sharpness and depth of field, and for manual focusing. So that photographers with vision problems can also see a clear and sharp image, the diopter value of the viewfinder system is important. Because of the modules built into the eyepiece rim for the eye-control system, however, Canon designers were unable to include a diopter adjustment system into the eyepiece of the EOS-3. The viewfinder system of the EOS-3 is designed with an overall diopter value of –1, which has been found to be ideal for the majority of users. Should you find that you cannot see the markings on the viewfinder screen absolutely clearly, then you may need to install a corrective eyepiece. Canon makes ten correction lenses, covering the range from –4 to +3 diopters. These lenses slip into place on the eyepiece and do not interfere with the operation of the eye-control system or the attachment of the standard rubber eyecup.

To determine if you need eyesight correction, take the lens off the camera (remembering to protect it with its rear cap) and look into the eyepiece with the camera pointed toward a light source (sky or interior wall, for example). If the standard eyesight correction works for you, then you will be able to see very clearly the elliptical area of autofocus as well as the central circle. If you find that you cannot see these marking clearly, then a trip to your eye doctor is in order. Most eye specialists have a set of diopter lenses with handles that you can hold between your eye and the camera viewfinder to determine which value provides the best vision. Once you have determined this, you can order the appropriate eyesight correction lens from your Canon dealer.

Focusing screens used by the EOS-3.

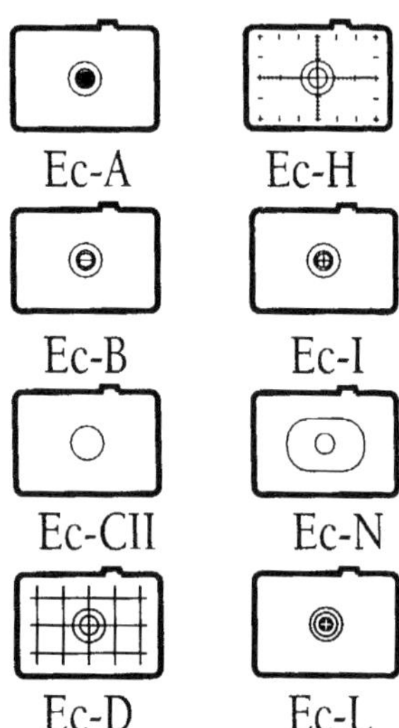

Focusing Screens

The EOS-3, which has its own dedicated screen, also accepts the EOS-1N's focusing screens, shown above. Screens are designed for easy use, depending on type of subject, lens focal length, and purpose. The EC-A (microprism), EC-B, and Ec-CII are used for general photography. The Ec-D is especially well suited for close-up or copy work and helps to keep the camera level. The Ec-H is effective for close-up photography and photomicrography. The EC-I is particularly useful for photomicrography and astrophotography; the Ec-L aids in manual focusing. The Ec-N, the standard EOS-1N focusing screen, has a fine spot-metering circle at the center and the 45-point area AF ellipse. The Ec-R (not shown) is the standard EOS-3 focusing screen. It allows a viewfinder image approximately one f/stop brighter than possible with the Ec-N. Custom Function 0 allows the proper metering compensation to be set when the screen is changed.

EOS-3 Basics

Loading the Film

Many beginners, and even some professionals, have gotten their first roll of film shot with a new camera back from the lab—and it's blank. This misloading of film so that it does not go through the camera has befallen all of us, but need not happen if sufficient care is exercised in loading the camera. The second roll of film will be more or less correctly exposed, but even then there may be problems with indistinct or blurred images. This happens in the photo business more often than you might think. Therefore, it is essential to learn how to properly load and operate your new camera prior to using it for important photographs.

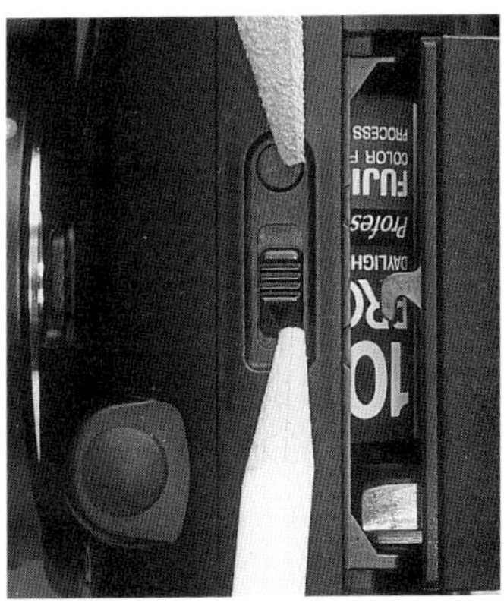

To open the camera back, press the release button and then slide the latch downward. The back will open immediately.

Film loading should always be done in the shade. In an emergency, you can use your body or a coat or jacket to create a small shady area. Be very careful that you never touch the camera shutter when putting the film cassette into the camera and pulling the film across. The shutter is made of overlapping leaves or blades—easily damaged by fingers. Replacing a shutter is a very expensive repair that you certainly want to avoid.

To open the back of the camera, press the locking button and slide the release latch located on the left end of the camera

When loading the film, pull the end of the film across until it lines up the with orange start mark. The film should lie as flat as possible and be evenly placed between the film guide rails.

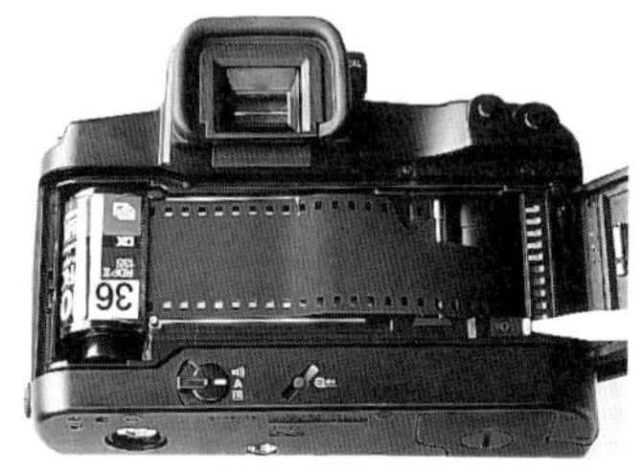

downward. This sounds more complicated than it is and will become second nature after a few minutes of practice. Now the back is released, and you can swing it open. You then insert the new film cassette into the chamber on the left side of the camera, placing the top end (the end without any spool protruding) in first and swinging the cassette downward into place. Use gentle finger pressure to make sure it seats itself and that the flat surface is on top; the film should then lie flat inside the camera on the two shiny metal film tracks. Take hold of the end of the film and gently draw it over toward the right until the end lines up with the red index mark on the camera body. If too much film protrudes from the cassette, take it back out of the camera and wind it in a little by turning the protruding spool end. Once you have the end of the film correctly aligned with the index, close the camera back. If the camera is turned off, turn it on, and the film will then be automatically wound forward to the first frame.

Verify proper film loading by looking at the LCD panel. If the film has loaded correctly, you will see a film cassette icon with film protruding and the frame counter will display 1; the ISO speed of the film will also be displayed. The cassette icon and frame counter number will remain visible even if the camera is switched off. If the film did not load properly, the cassette icon will flash and no number will appear in the frame counter display. If this happens, open the back and make sure the film is pulled to the right far enough to line up with the index mark. Don't be dismayed if you occasionally misload a roll of film. One of us confesses to doing so occasionally even after more than 30 years of photography!

Choosing the Film

Two basic questions must be answered prior to making your film choice. First, do you want prints or slides, and second, do you want color or black and white? There are no right and wrong answers to these questions, just personal preferences. Each photographer sees differently, and that inner vision is best expressed in certain films and in the way they are presented.

The choice of film can also depend on what you are photographing. As an example, you may be asked to photograph a wedding. The majority of people want their wedding photos in color, but black and white is becoming increasingly popular. Whichever you use, though, you would want to use negative film so that friends and family can easily get prints, as from a baptism or birthday, for example.

You may be thinking that you can get always get prints from slides—and this is true. Prints from slides, however, cost more and not every lab can do a really good job with them. We advise that when prints are the desired final product, it always makes more sense to use print film to take the photos.

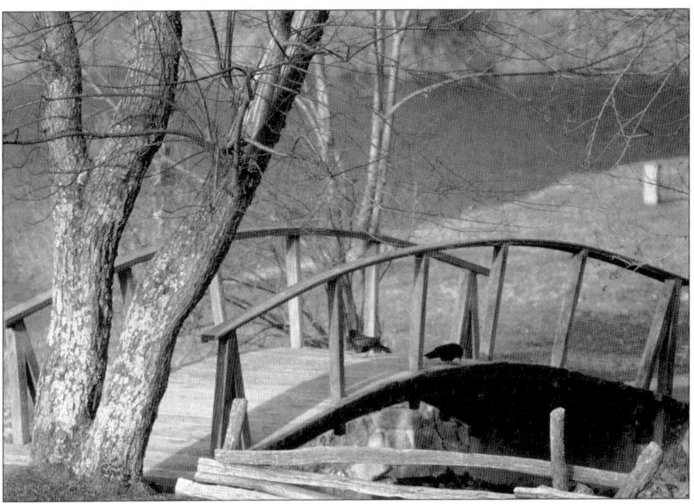

This photo is packed with information from corner to corner. Fill the frame, include a range of highlight and shadows, and use perspective to create an interesting composition. Photo by Bob Shell.

The pros and cons of films can be summarized as follows: Slide films require a smaller contrast range in your subject matter and must be exposed very accurately. Deviations of 0.5 EV (see discussion below) can clearly be seen in slide films. Visual evaluation of slides is easier than with negatives because the colors are not reversed. Negative films have much greater exposure latitude and carry a greater contrast range. Their exposure latitude can be so great that a usable print may be made from a negative underexposed by two stops or overexposed by three stops. With negative films, however, the color quality and sharpness depend a great deal on the lab.

Exposure Value (EV)
The exposure value (EV) is a numerical value that applies to a specific level of light. Thus, a particular EV does not indicate specific shutter speeds or aperture values, but a set of both that will each produce an equivalent exposure on film. For example, 1/250 + f/2, 1/125 + f/2.8, 1/60 + f/4, 1/30 + f/5.6, and 1/15 + f/8 all give the same exposure on the film—all have the same exposure value.

Reciprocity

Reciprocity is the characteristic of film that varies its response to light at different exposure durations. At very long or very short exposures you may need to add additional exposure to the film to get proper exposure, and with color films the different layers may respond differently so that filtration may be necessary for proper color rendition. Check the information sheets for the film you plan to use to find out if reciprocity correction will be necessary at very long or very short exposure times, and use the manufacturer's recommendations as the starting points for your own experimentation to determine how much correction produces the look you want in the photos.

Film Speed

Low-speed films (ISO speeds of 25 or 50) are extremely fine in grain and very sharp with very high brilliance and color saturation. They have very narrow exposure latitude in most cases. The danger of image blurring from camera shake is much greater with these films unless a sturdy tripod is always used.

Medium-speed films (ISO 100 to 200) are fine grained and sharp, with good brilliance and color saturation. Contrast and exposure range are a satisfactory compromise.

High-speed films with ISO of 400 to 3200 become grainier as speed increases and show a corresponding loss of sharpness. Brilliance and color saturation also generally decrease as speed increases. But when the light levels are low, these films are the best ones to reach for.

If you are going to photograph people, you may want to use the special portrait films from several makers, with ISO speeds in the 160 and 400 range. For brilliant landscapes or architecture, you may want a film with more color saturation and contrast, and an ISO 50 film may be better. For sports and wildlife photography, you may find that you require a fast film to be able to use the telephoto lenses this sort of photography requires, and a film of ISO 400 or even some of the new ISO 800 films may be ideal.

Setting the Film Speed

With the Canon EOS-3, the setting of the ISO speed for the film can be done either automatically (used most of the time) or manually. For automatic setting, you need do nothing. The camera is supplied from the factory set to read the information from the film cassette (DX code) and set the camera accordingly for speeds from ISO 25 up to ISO 5000. Film ISO can be input manually by pressing the AF button and the exposure compenstion button at the same time. This is marked on the camera by two arrows with ISO in between. When you do this, you will see DX appear on the LCD panel. You can scroll through the ISO number available for manual input by turning the Main Dial while keeping these two buttons depressed. The range runs from ISO 6 to ISO 6400, so it should cover any reasonable need.

Because almost every film made in the world today is supplied in cassettes with DX coding, most photographers will leave

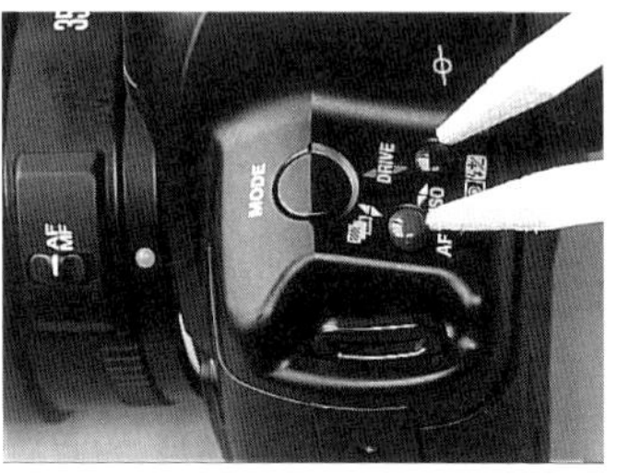

You can manually set the ISO speed by pressing the AF mode button and the exposure compensation button, and turning the Main Dial. These buttons are well marked with arrows and the ISO indicator.

the setting on DX. Even if you load your own film into empty cassettes, you can buy both precoded cassettes and DX code stickers for a variety of film speeds.

If for some reason you find that you often need to set ISO manually, you may use Custom Function 3 to cause the camera to retain its manually set ISO speed when film is changed. If you do not do this, the camera reverts to DX automatic function each time the film is changed.

Safeguarding High-Speed Film When Traveling

Films with ISO speeds higher than ISO 400 may be damaged by x-ray scanning equipment used in airports. If you anticipate needing to use very high-speed film during travel, buy the film at your destination and have it processed prior to flying home.

Motorized Film Advance

The Canon EOS-3 is a high-performance camera that offers several user-controlled options in the film advance. The film loading, rewinding, and frame-to-frame advance are all fully automatic. If you simultaneously press the AF and mode buttons, you can switch between single-frame advance and continuous advance with the Main Dial. For most photographs most of the time, single-frame advance will be the film advance mode of choice. In this mode of operation, you must press the shutter release each time you want to take a photograph. When photographing sports or other rapidly changing situations, you will most likely find that continuous film advance meets your needs better. In this mode, the camera will take photos as rapidly as possible as long as you keep the shutter release button depressed.

When you have the AF mode set to One Shot AF or are using manual focus, the fastest speed at which the camera can operate is 4.3 frames per second (fps); when set to AI Servo AF, the maximum speed is 3.3 fps. These numbers refer to the basic camera operating speed without motor accessories.

With the addition of the PB-E2 motor drive booster and the NiMH battery pack, both optional accessories, the maximum speed increases to seven frames per second. If you use alkaline AA cells instead of the NiMH pack, the speed drops to six frames per second in One Shot AF or five frames per second in AI Servo AF. With either energy source, the PB-E2 booster offers two speeds—H (for High) with the two speeds just mentioned, and L (for Low), which provides three frames per second regardless of the AF setting. Additionally, the booster makes an excellent handgrip for vertical shooting, offering its own shutter release button, Main Dial, and AE and FEL buttons, as well as an AF sensor area control button.

The Canon EOS-3 can also be used with the motor drive booster E1, developed for the EOS-1 and EOS-1N. The E1 provides similar performance with alkaline AA cells, but cannot be used with a NiMH pack.

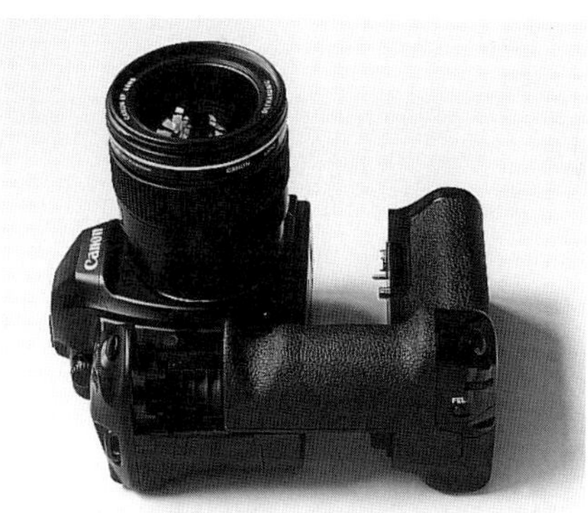

The PB-E2 power drive booster is attached to the camera after the removal of the protective cover on the bottom of the cover.

Film Rewinding

As you would expect, the Canon EOS-3 rewinds the film automatically at the end of each roll. You have several possible ways of operating it, however. In the basic default setting, the film rewinds at the end of each roll as soon as the last photo is taken. During rewind, the motion of the film is indicated by flashing bars on the LCD panel; when the film is fully rewound, the cassette icon on the LCD panel flashes. Only then is it safe to open the back and remove the film cassette.

You can rewind a partially used roll of film at any time by simply pressing the manual rewind button with your thumbnail or a pointed object. This button is recessed to prevent its accidental activation. Also, with Custom Function 2, you can set the rewind system so that the short edge of the film (the film leader) is left protruding from the cassette. This is useful if you rewind a partially used roll with the intention of using the rest later on. If you do this, use a permanent marker to indicate on the film edge how many exposures have been taken, and when you reload this film cassette, advance the camera one extra frame to prevent overlapping film frames. Be sure to tell the processing lab about this marking so that their automatic cutting machinery will not cut through your photos on the latter part of the roll.

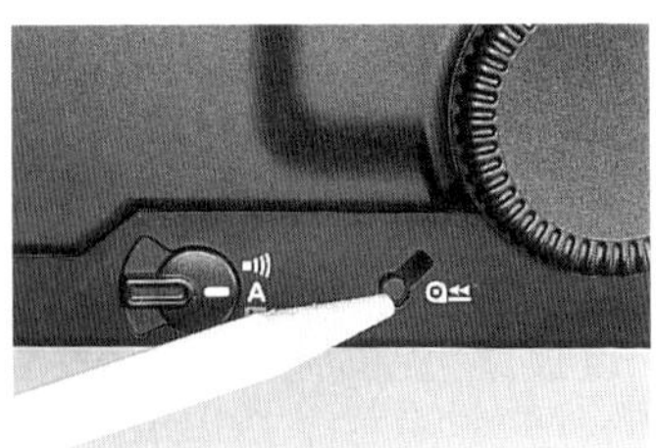

The pointer shows the button for selecting manual film rewinding.

Custom Function 1 offers four options in controlling the rewind. You can set it for regular rewind with automatic start or regular rewind with manual start, as well as a somewhat slower quiet rewind, again with either automatic or manual start. This allows you to pick the rewind speed and sound level you want. At times you may wish to set the camera for manual start of the rewind to avoid the whine of rewinding intruding on solemn occasions. You can then go outside or into a hallway and rewind there.

Self-Timer

You will not find the internationally standardized pictogram for the self-timer (a stylized clock face) on any button on the EOS-3, but it is very easy to access. Just press the mode and metering selection buttons at the same time. While holding down these two buttons and rotating the Main Dial, scroll through the drive indicators on the LCD panel. You will note that there are two self-timer selections marked with 10 and 2; these select exposure delays of ten and two seconds respectively. When you activate the self-timer by pressing on the shutter release button, the LCD data panel shows a countdown and the red light on the front of the camera flashes, slowly at first and then rapidly during the last second prior to exposure. This allows you to know precisely when the camera will fire for those times you want to get yourself in the picture. If you decide you want to cancel the self-timer cycle before the camera fires, you can do so by turning the camera off with the main power switch on the back. When you turn the camera back on, you must then press the two buttons again and use the Main Dial to switch the camera out of the self-timer mode.

The self-timer can be used with any Canon-dedicated flash unit. If no tripod is available, you can use tables, windowsills, banisters, tree limbs, and similar supports to hold the camera. When setting up the camera for photos with the self-timer, it is important to select an AF sensor that will be an important element of the composition, or to switch to manual focus to ensure the focus stays on the desired area. When you are using the camera on a tripod and your eye will not be at the viewfinder during the exposure, be sure to take off the eyecup and replace it with the eyepiece shutter on the camera strap to keep stray light from entering the viewfinder and adversely affecting the exposure. This is most important when there is a strong light source directly behind the camera.

The self-timer can also be helpful in allowing vibration to damp down prior to exposure when making macro photos or working with long telephotos, and can be used along with mirror prerelease via Custom Function 12-1. When set this way, the mirror goes up and locks in place when the shutter release button is pressed, and also starts the self-timer. To take the photo when the self-timer is not in use, you must press once to lift the mirror and a second time to take the photo. Remember that once set, Custom Function 12-1 will retain its setting unless you manually reset it to 0 or return the camera to all default settings with the CLEAR button.

Mirror Prerelease

Mirror prerelease can be useful for photography in which the most critical image sharpness is an important consideration, such as when the image will be enlarged up to poster size. A sturdy professional tripod is also an essential for getting such image quality. In order not to shake the camera when tripping the shutter, you should use either the Remote Switch RS-80N3 or the self-timer. In any case, the mirror returns to its normal position for viewing after the exposure. If you wish to cancel a long exposure while it is in progress, you can do so by switching the camera off with the main switch on the back, which will cause the shutter to close and the mirror to return to viewing position. Also, if you trip the mirror prerelease and do not make the actual exposure within thirty seconds, the mirror will return to viewing position and must be raised again by pressing the shutter release button.

Mirror prerelease works best with manual focus, although you can use it with autofocus. You can also use it with any exposure mode except DEP.

Date Back

The camera back of the EOS-3 can be removed and replaced with the Date Back DB-E2, which allows printing of the date onto the film while taking photos. This can be in the form of year/month/day, day/hour/minute, month/day/year, or day/month/year. The built-in clock is programmed to keep track of date and time through the year 2019. The Date Back DB-E2 is equipped with the Quick Control Dial and switch, and film window, just like the standard camera back, but also has a small LCD panel. Under this LCD panel are three small buttons—MODE, SELECT and SET—for setting and controlling the functions of the Date Back. These buttons are used in combination to set or change the date information, or to change the display to — — —, in which no imprinting will occur. The date is printed directly onto the film and appears in the lower right corner of the image (assuming a horizontal image). On light areas or very bright areas, it may be difficult to see the imprinted information, so try to keep a darker part of the subject in this area.

It is important to remember to turn off the imprinting feature when it is not needed so that it does not intrude into and ruin images. The Date Back is more useful for scientific and technical applications than for general photography, although it can be useful as a memory-jogging reminder for vacation trips.

Holding the Camera and Photographic Technique

If in spite of highly sophisticated AF technology and image stabilization you are still getting unsharp photos, it probably is your holding technique that is at fault. Forget the stylish posings of "photographers" seen at resorts and in the movies, with their never-ending rolls of film and impossible telephoto lenses. Proper camera holding is not so impressive, but will result in much improved photos. Your percentage of sharp photos will increase dramatically if you follow these suggestions:

- ❏ Good contact with a solid support is important, and this will usually be the ground. Most photographers find that standing with one foot somewhat forward of the other results in greater stability. Your arms and hands holding the camera should not be stiff and cramped but relaxed. In this position, the camera is brought to your face resting against your nose and brow—right brow if you are right-eyed and left brow if you use your left eye to view. Your right thumb should rest in the hollow between the AE lock button and the Quick Control Dial, while your right index finger rests on the shutter release button. The remaining fingers of your right hand wrap around the hand grip. Your left hand will support the camera and lens, with the camera body resting on your palm and your thumb and index fingers resting on the zoom ring (if it is a zoom lens). Both elbows should be drawn in against your sides. This is generally the best way to hold your camera when taking horizontal photographs.

- For vertical photographs, there are two different holds depending on whether the camera is fitted with the PB-E2 power drive booster. If it is not fitted with the booster, begin with the hold described above and move your left hand under the end of the camera as your right hand rotates the hand grip upward until the camera axis is vertical; your left elbow should be pressed firmly against your side. The power booster makes the vertical grip almost identical to the horizontal and increases comfort in prolonged shooting situations.

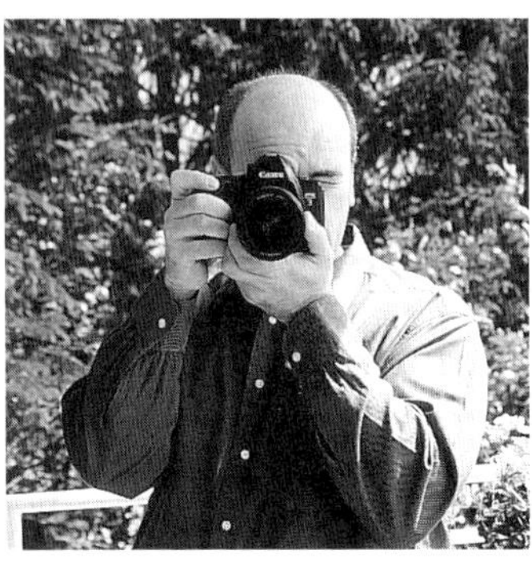

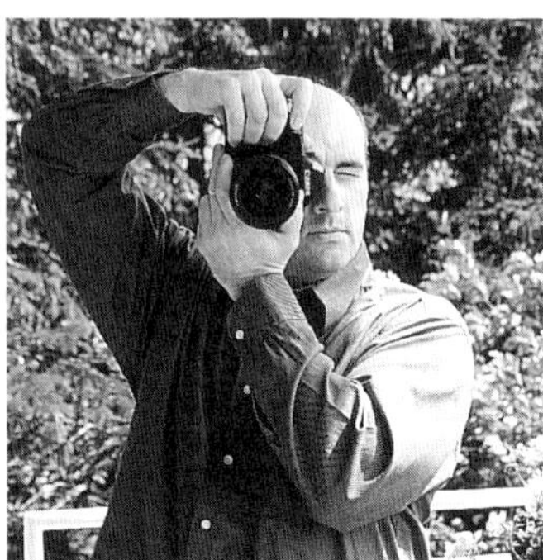

The recommended way to hold the camera for taking horizontal (left) and vertical (right) pictures.

- Regardless of the hold used, it is best to breathe normally until just before taking the photograph, when you should inhale and then exhale and hold, and at that point trip the shutter. If conditions make this sort of stance impossible, you can modify this into a kneeling position and still have good stability. Or, you can carry along a monopod or use naturally available supports to steady your camera.
- There is a rule of thumb that your shutter speed, when you're handholding the camera, should be approximate to the focal length of your lens for sharp images. For a 50mm lens, this would be 1/50 second; typically, though, handholding at shutter speeds below 1/60 second is not recommended. This rule of thumb is remarkably accurate for most people. It will not guarantee sharp images, but it will reduce the number of blurred ones. If your film speed allows, of course, always move to faster shutter speeds to increase your number of sharp images.

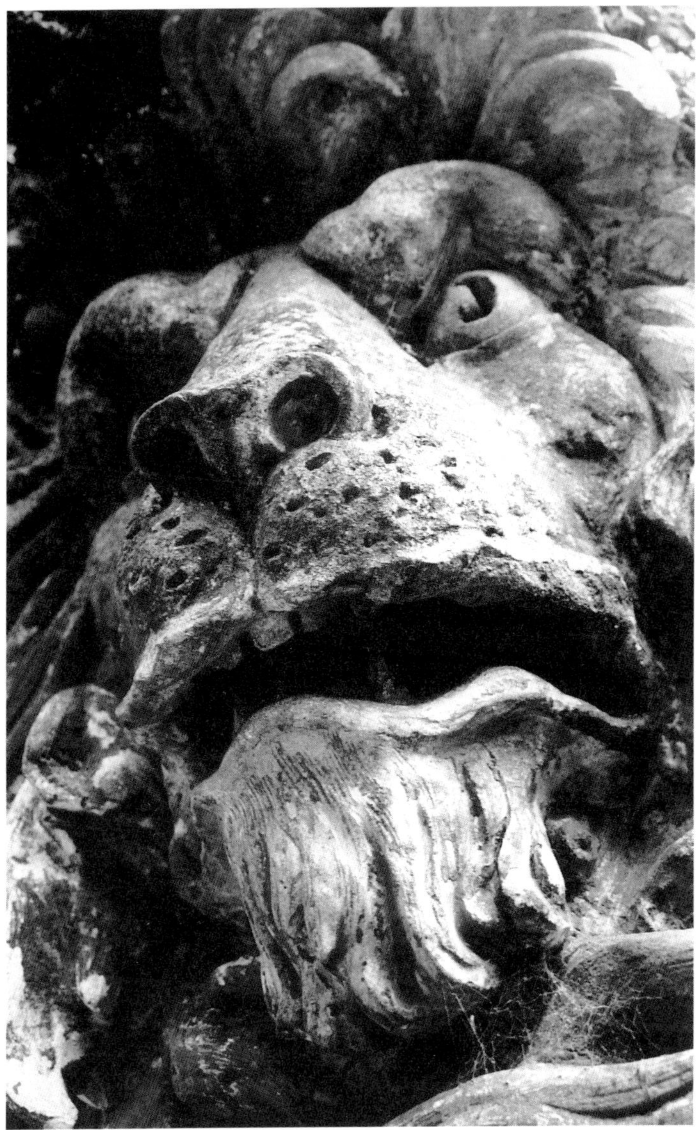

The most successful travel photos are often taken from an unusual vantage point. Here, the photographer incorporated a pigeon's eye view of a sculpture in London. Photo by Bob Shell.

Focusing

The EOS-3 and Canon EF lenses offer a choice of full autofocus (AF) or manual focus. Each type of focusing has its advantages and limitations. This chapter discusses the ways to use each type of focusing for best photographic results.

The Autofocus System

The Canon EOS-3 probably has the best AF system in the world. To be such a superlative system, it must produce very precise focusing of the lens, because every lens must achieve its maximum sharpness within only a very thin image plane (where the film rests in the camera). Focusing is, by definition, adjusting the lens so that the sharpest possible image is formed on the film. This is done by shifting the position of the lens, or some of its elements, along the axis of the lens.

The 45 AF focusing points, shown on the EOS-3 viewfinder.

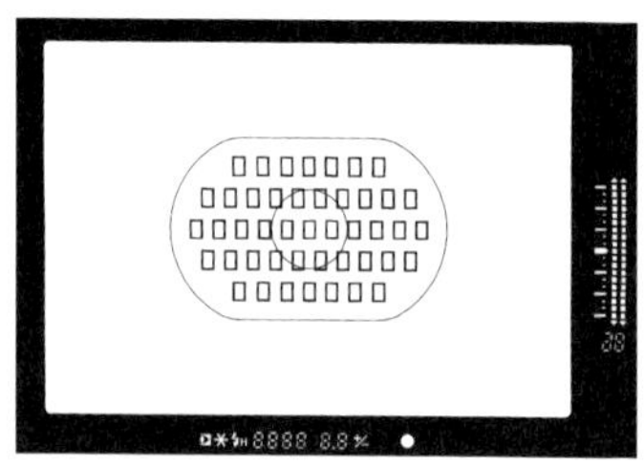

In addition, the EOS-3 AF system establishes a new world record, as the first camera with 45 separate AF sensors. Canon speaks of this as a wide focusing field, and that is not inaccurate because the 45 AF sensors form a focusing field that constitutes a quarter of the image area, with a pixel density of 10,724 pixels. The number of pixels is significant, because the AF module converts light into electrical signals. The Complementary Metal Oxide Semiconductor (CMOS) sensors in the EOS-3 can generate signals ten times as fast as the Multi-BASIS (Base-Stored Image

Sensor) used in other EOS cameras in their AF systems. Additionally, the EOS-3 has an ultra-fast 32-bit microprocessor (clock frequency 24,576 cycles per second), with substantially improved signal processing software. This makes the system so fast that it can follow subjects and ensure absolute sharpness at the maximum speed of seven frames per second (fps) (with the PB-E2 power drive booster and the NP-E2 NiMH battery pack). The increased density of the AF sensors also facilitates maintaining focus on moving subjects. The AF sensors start to work almost instantly due to the rapid response of the eye-control system and its ability to follow the smallest eye movements; this produces the most rapid response, allowing the EOS-3 to track a subject moving at 24 miles per hour (40 km/hr). The AF sensors can also be activated automatically, with the area of focus determined by the camera's computer, or it can be selected manually. In every case, the active sensor is indicated by red-lighted rectangles on the viewfinder screen, as long as One Shot AF mode is in use.

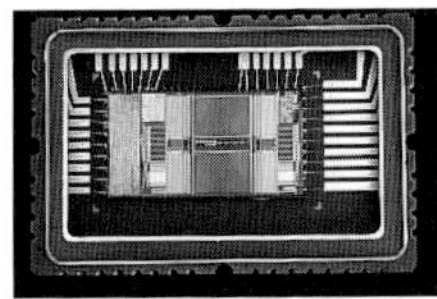

Area AF CMOS sensor.

Calibration of the Eye-Control Autofocus

Canon's eye-control feature detects the movement of the eye's pupil as it looks through the camera's eyepiece. With the EOS-3, Canon has now refined this system to operate well when the EOS-3 is turned for vertical shooting. In this new system, eight IREDs (infrared-emitting diodes) shine their beams into the photographer's eye, and the reflected infrared is decoded by a sensor system and new software to tell the camera's AF system precisely where the photographer is looking. In addition to this physical redesign, the response time of the system was lowered to only 67 milliseconds. The eye control is factory set with an average calibration, but each camera user will need to calibrate it again to his or her eye.

The EOS-3 has three separate memory sets, so it can be calibrated for up to three different users or three ways for one individual user—if, for example, that user wanted to make one calibration with just the eye, a second one with eyeglasses or contact lenses, and a third with sunglasses. With special types of eyeglasses, however, such as silver coatings or strong polarization, the eye-control system will not work.

To use the eye control, turn it on by moving the eye-control switch to the I position. (In the O position, the eye-control system is switched off.) To calibrate the eye control, first turn the knob on the top right of the prism housing to the position marked CAL. You will then see CAL-1—the calibration channel—displayed on the LCD panel and inside the viewfinder below the image area. The number is the calibration channel. You can scroll from CAL-1 to CAL-2 and CAL-3 by rotating the Main Dial. Once you have selected the channel you wish to calibrate, you will begin with the camera held for horizontal image orientation. You will see an area to the right of the AF sensor ellipse that is blinking red. Look directly at this flashing red area and press the shutter release button once. The flashing area should stop flashing and remain red. Then a section of the left area will begin to flash, and you should look at this without moving your head and once again press the shutter release button while looking fixedly at the flashing red. Next, repeat these steps for the upper and lower areas, which

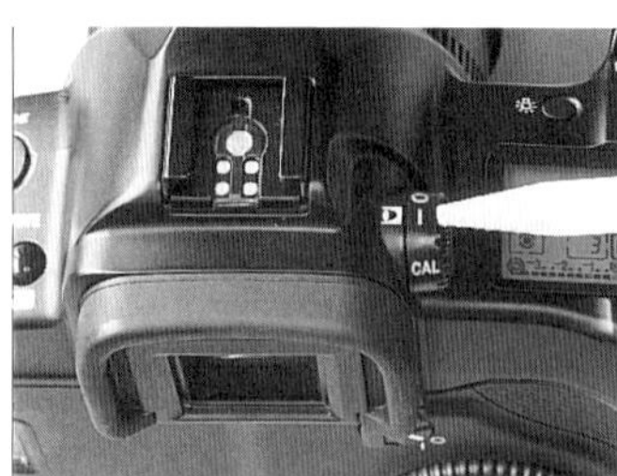

To turn on the eye control, turn the knob until it is in the I position; to calibrate the eye control, turn the knob to the CAL position. In the O position, eye control is off.

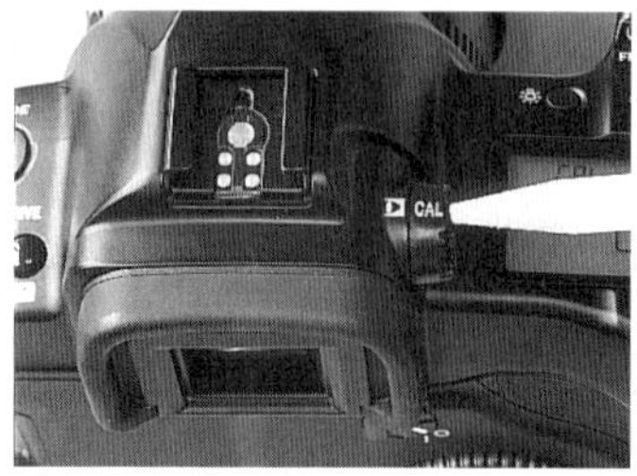

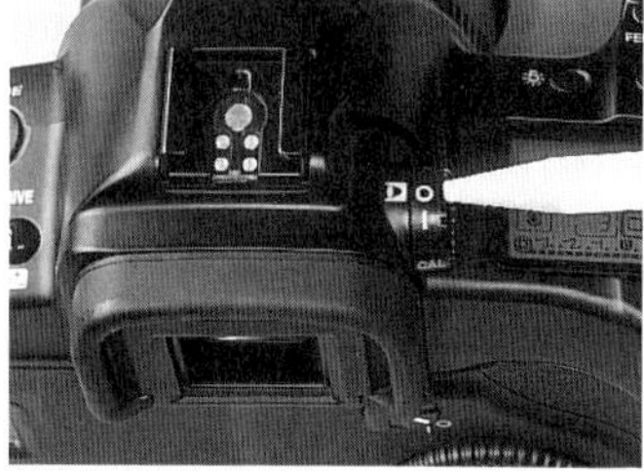

will flash. If you have been successful in this first calibration, you will see the LCD displays showing END-1. After this, turn the camera to its vertical position and lightly press the shutter release button. The calibration process is repeated. If this calibration has been successful, you will see END-1 again. It is a good idea to repeat the whole process several times in different light levels, because the system will continue to fine tune itself each time a new calibration is added. The last calibration is automatically used unless you set the dial to CAL and change it.

When calibrating the eye control, do so in a variety of light levels to achieve the best possible performance. Sit calmly while doing the calibration and keep your eye in the same position. Sit erect and look directly at the flashing area—not past it into the distance. Do not let strong light shine on or into the eyepiece, as this can adversely affect calibration. And, if you wear eyeglasses, be sure they are seated properly on your face.

The AF Modes

The AF system of the Canon EOS-3 is turned on whenever the AF/FM switch on the lens is in the AF position. The EOS-3 offers two AF modes—One Shot AF and AI (artificial intelligence) Servo AF—which can be switched manually. While pressing the AF button (marked AF and located on the top left of the camera), you can use the Main Dial to switch between these two modes, and the mode you choose is indicated on the external LCD panel. One Shot AF means AF with sharpness priority; the camera shutter will not fire until the AF system has locked onto a subject and brought the lens into sharp focus. On the other hand, in AI Servo AF mode the camera will constantly adjust focus to track a moving subject and focus as sharply as possible on it, but the shutter can be released at any time, even if the sharpest focus has not been achieved. Each of these modes works best for specific photographic situations. One Shot AF, in general, is good for static or slowly moving subjects, while AI Servo AF generally works best for subjects in more rapid motion.

One Shot AF

In this AF mode, most photographic subjects will be sharply focused. It is good for portraits, figure studies, landscapes, still lifes—any situation in which the subject does not move or moves slowly; sharpness is the priority.

Activate autofocus in this mode by pressing halfway on the shutter release button and waiting until focus is confirmed in the viewfinder (or by the beeper when that is turned on). Once focus is achieved, you can press the shutter release the rest of the way and take a photo at any time. A flashing AF indicator in the viewfinder indicates the AF system is unable to establish focus; this can be caused by lack of subject contrast or by very bright reflections on shiny surfaces. In such a situation, release the shutter release button and use the eye control or manual control to direct the focus at a different part of your subject, taking care to pick an area at the same distance as your original choice of focus. Because of the large area in which focus can be set, measuring a full 0.6 x 0.3 inches (15 x 8 mm), it should be possible to find an alternate area of focus. Remember also that the 21 metering areas are weighted toward the active AF sensor, so the choice should not be made in unusually dark or light areas of your subject.

AI Servo AF

This AF mode is the best choice for photographing most subjects moving at moderate to high speed. The system is activated by

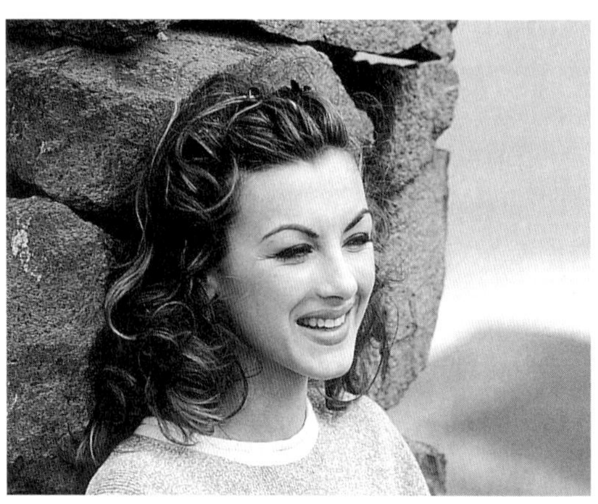

One Shot AF mode is perfect for portraits.

half pressure on the shutter release button, as described above, but in this case the AF system locks onto the subject as soon as the subject moves. The subject is then tracked automatically while moving across the area of the AF sensors, going from sensor to sensor—one reason the system can track moving subjects even at the speed of seven fps. In practice, because of the extremely fast AF system and the weighting of the metering to the main subject, this mode can produce outstanding images of any sort of moving subject. With subjects moving toward or away from the camera, the camera's built-in computer can predict the location from frame to frame, and can calculate the location between the time that focus is achieved and the camera shutter actually fires.

In the AI Servo AF mode, the camera will fire whether focus has been achieved or not, so it is possible to trip the shutter before the camera has had time to focus the first time. The focus confirmation signal and beeper are switched off in this mode of

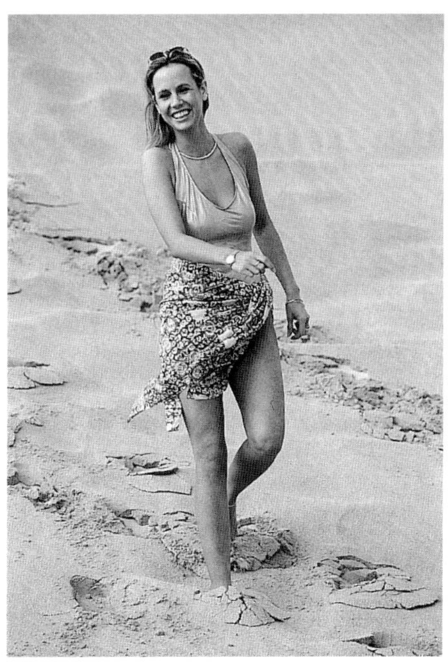

AI Servo mode is ideal for moving subjects in either bright or dim light.

operation. In addition, the active AF sensor indicator does not light up. With Custom Function 4, the EOS-3 can be programmed so that autofocus is activated with the AE lock button.

Managing the AF System

The AF system of the EOS-3 is a passive system. This means that it responds to the brightness and contrast of the subject and reacts to the ambient light the subject is reflecting. Because of this characteristic, the AF system works best with brightly illuminated and/or contrasty subjects and can fail with dull or low-contrast subjects. Smooth, untextured surfaces can also be a source of AF error. Highly reflective subjects can cause problems for the AF system by blinding the sensors with glare. The best choice in any of these situations is to pick a substitute subject at the same distance as the one you wish to focus on and focus there, holding the focus with One Shot AF and keeping the shutter release button depressed halfway.

Choosing AF Sensors

The AF ellipse, placed centrally in the viewfinder, forms a field in which 45 individual AF sensors perform their work. These sensors can be chosen automatically, manually, or by eye control. In each case, the active AF sensor or sensors is indicated in the viewfinder with lighted red rectangles.

Automatic choice of AF sensors is activated by setting the eye-control switch on the side of the prism housing to the O position. Simply press the shutter release button halfway down and the AF system is switched on. The camera will select an AF area based on information programmed into the camera's CPU. If the camera has been set for manual selection of the AF sensor, you must press the button for AF sensor selection (far right on upper back of the camera, and marked with a group of small rectangles) and use the Main Dial and/or Quick Control Dial to scroll through the choices on the LCD until a single, large, elongated rectangle is displayed. This indicates automatic AF sensor selection and is the default mode.

With the automatic choice of the AF sensors, the camera

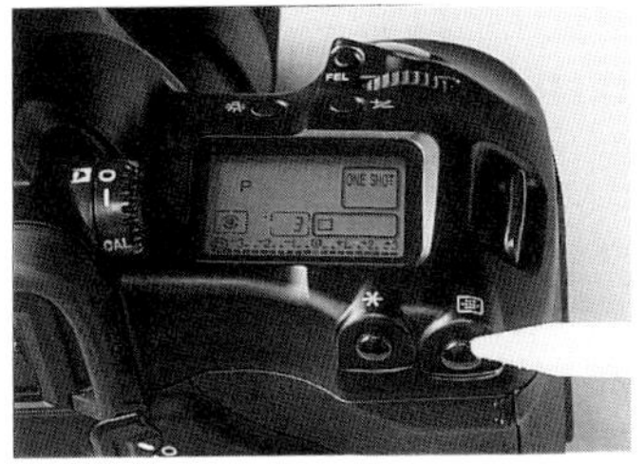

The pointer shows the focusing point selector button.

selects an area as long as a good subject is in the area of the AF ellipse. It is very easy to get your intended subject within the ellipse, as it covers 23% of the image area. The automatic programming will have the camera choose to focus on the subject within the ellipse that is closest to the camera, working on the assumption that your intended subject is usually the closest subject to the camera. If, in fact, the closest subject is not your desired point of focus, you need to switch to manual or eye-controlled selection of the AF sensor.

Manually selecting the desired AF sensor is simple; just press and release the button for AF sensor selection. With the Main Dial (horizontal choice) and/or Quick Control Dial (vertical choice), scroll through the selection of available AF sensor areas until the one you want one is indicated on the viewing screen in the viewfinder.

With the Quick Control Dial, it is also possible to select the AF sensor only by setting Custom Function 11-2. This allows use only of the central horizontal line of sensors, however. Sometimes you will see more than one AF sensor area light up—or even alternate with one another. In practice, though, only one AF sensor will be active at any time.

Manual Control in the AF Area

When you are using manual sensor selection, there may be times when you do not want all 45 AF sensors active. In this instance, you can use Custom Function 17 (see next page) and change the programming so that only the central AF sensor areas are active. This makes manual control of the AF area much faster. Custom Function 13 also has the option of linking spot metering to one of the 11 AF sensor areas.

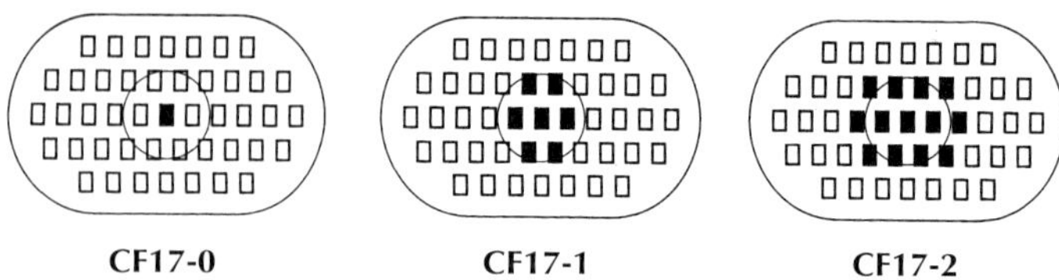

These diagrams show the options for enlarging the focusing area with Custom Function 17.

Setting the Brightness of the AF Area Indicator Lights

With Custom Function 10, you can set the brightness of the AF indicator lights manually. Position 0 is the standard setting and will be correct for most people most of the time. You have a choice of how the display operates: Position 1 switches off the lights completely, and there is no indication in the viewfinder of the active AF sensor; Position 2 turns the AF sensor lights on; in Position 3, the active sensor lights only briefly, but with maximum brightness.

Tips on AF Sensors

With automatic or manual choice of the AF sensors, the eye control must be switched off (switch set to O). Otherwise, the eye control is active and the eye indicator in the viewfinder is lighted. The AF/MF switch on the lens can be in either position, because even when manual focusing is in use the AF indicators will light up when focus is achieved and can assist manual focusing.

The 45 AF sensors are in three types, with three different levels of sensitivity. The greatest sensitivity is the one central cross-shaped sensor. The whole sensor will work with lenses of f/4 or faster, whereas the vertical line sensor making up part of the cross will still function with lenses as slow as f/8. This means that for the first time lenses with apertures this small can still work with autofocus and lenses mounted on teleconverters. This capability is unique to the EOS-3, as no other camera will provide autofocus with lenses as slow as f/8. Around this central sensor are six other cross-shaped AF sensors, which work with f/2.8 or faster lenses. As with the central cross-shaped sensor, the vertical arms of these sensors are more sensitive working with slower lenses.

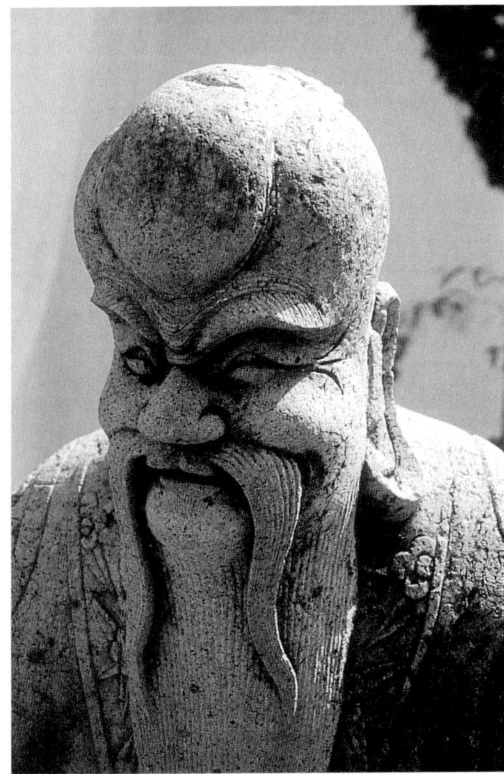

The autofocus system of the EOS-3 is rapid and accurate, allowing the photographer to concentrate on the composition.

The remaining 38 AF sensors are shaped in vertical bars and have a sensitivity allowing lenses as slow as f/5.6 to activate them. The high sensitivity of all the sensors, combined with their rapid response, contributes to the AF speed and accuracy of the EOS-3 when used with zoom lenses or lenses combined with teleconverters. With faster lenses, the performance is even more rapid and surer.

Focusing and Composition

The large AF ellipse takes up 23% of the image area, so the system can focus on different objects. Often, when new photographers look through the viewfinder, they tend to put their main subject in the center of the frame. From the point of view of picture design, this is not always the best idea. The broad focusing area of the EOS-3, in fact, makes it easy to place subjects more to the sides, often working with the classical composition formula of the golden mean. In such cases, it is easy to activate one of the off-center AF sensors, either manually or by eye control, and bring the lens to focus by pressing halfway down on the shutter release button. Once focus has been found, it can be held by maintaining pressure on the shutter release button while any necessary small adjustments in composition are made. So long as you maintain pressure on the shutter release button, this specific focusing distance will be locked. This also locks the exposure setting as well as the focus, and weights the exposure toward the AF sensor used when evaluative metering is used. If spot or center-weighted averaging metering is used, the exposure will be determined based on the image area. If you wish to store the information from the spot meter or from center-weighted average metering, you can lock this reading by pressing the AE lock button and holding it while simultaneously pressing the shutter release button halfway down. This may sound complicated, but with practice it will become second nature to hold pressure on the shutter release button with your right index finger while using your thumb to press the AE lock button. All this works, of course, only in One Shot AF mode.

In AI Servo AF mode, the EOS-3 can be programmed so that focus can be locked by pressure on the AE lock button. This is done with Custom Function 4.

See the chapter on image composition for a complete discussion of this topic.

Manual Focusing

Although the Canon EOS-3 undoubtedly has a superb, highly responsive AF system, there are often photographic situations in which manual focus may be preferred. This can be because the lens does not offer autofocus, as with a few specialty Canon lenses such as the TS (tilt-shift) lenses. Also, certain accessories, such as the bellows unit, will deactivate the autofocus. When you encounter such situations, you have two options: you can focus visually or you can use the AF system to confirm focus. In both such cases, if the lens is equipped with an AF/MF switch it must be in the MF position.

In manual focusing, the view on the viewing screen is adequate for most lenses. You simply turn the focusing ring on the lens until your main subject looks as sharp as possible. Generally, you will find it best to focus past the subject and then turn back to fine tune the adjustment. You can focus almost anywhere on the standard viewing screen supplied with the EOS-3. This makes it easy to concentrate on image design.

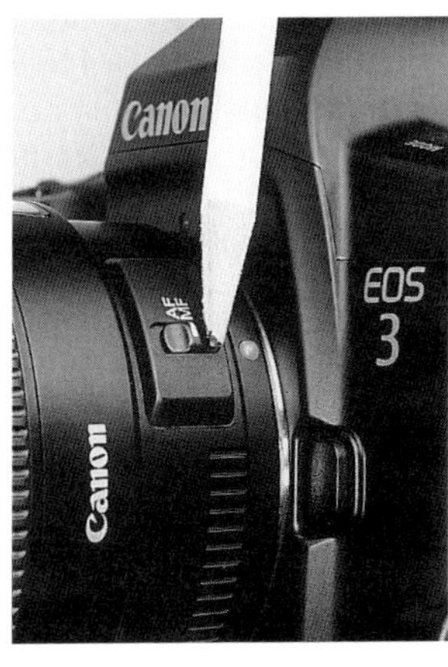

You can switch to manual focusing by moving the AF/MF switch to the MF position.

Manual focusing with electronic focusing assistance is equally easy. Just do not forget to set the AF/MF switch to MF. To activate the AF system, you must press halfway down on the shutter release button. You can then use the green in-focus indicator in the viewfinder, together with the focusing ring on the camera, to achieve the best possible focus.

The greatest focusing accuracy in dimmer light will be obtained by placing the central cross-shaped sensor (in the very center of the circle on the viewing screen) on the subject.

Remember that a correctly adjusted viewfinder is crucial for accurate manual focusing. Even though you may not need a corrective eyepiece lens for general photography, you may need one for manual focusing if you cannot see the markings on the viewing screen with absolute sharpness. It is easiest to determine this without distraction from subjects, so remove the lens and point the camera body toward an evenly illuminated wall and see whether the markings are clear and sharp. If they are not, a visit to your eye doctor may be in order to determine what corrective lens are needed for the camera eyepiece.

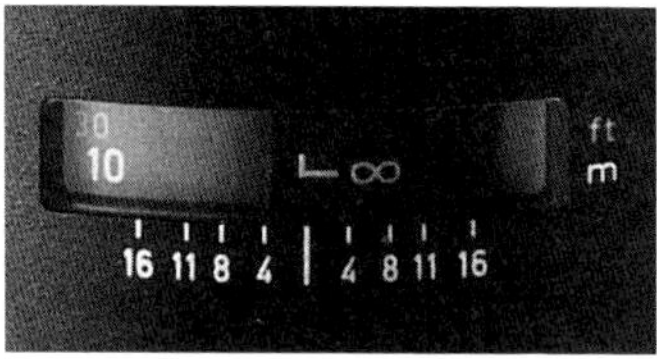

The depth-of-field scale shown focused at infinity.

Hyperfocal Distance and Depth of Field

The sharpness of most lenses is greatest when the lens is focused to a specific distance. With most lenses, this is infinity. There is a range of acceptable sharpness, however, known as depth of field. At any given lens aperture, there is what is called a hyperfocal distance—the distance at which the lens is focused for maximum depth of field. This will begin at a specific distance and carry through to infinity.

As an example, a 50 mm lens set to f/16 should be focused at 15.5 feet (4.7 m) to achieve its hyperfocal distance. Set in this way, everything from about 7.7 feet (2.34 m) to infinity will be acceptably sharply focused.

On lenses with a depth-of-field scale—generally not zoom lenses—the hyperfocal setting is done easily by turning the focusing ring until the infinity symbol lines up with the aperture number on the right side of the scale, to which the lens is set. On the left side of that scale the same aperture number will line up with the closest distance at which focus will be sharp. Unfortunately, on many lenses, and particularly on zoom lenses, it has not been practical to include depth-of-field scales. (See page 83 in exposure methods chapter for additional discussion of depth of field.)

Depth-of-Field Preview Button

If you look at the camera body from the front, the depth of field preview button is on the left of the lens mount at about the 8 o'clock position. It is used to visually preview the depth of field.

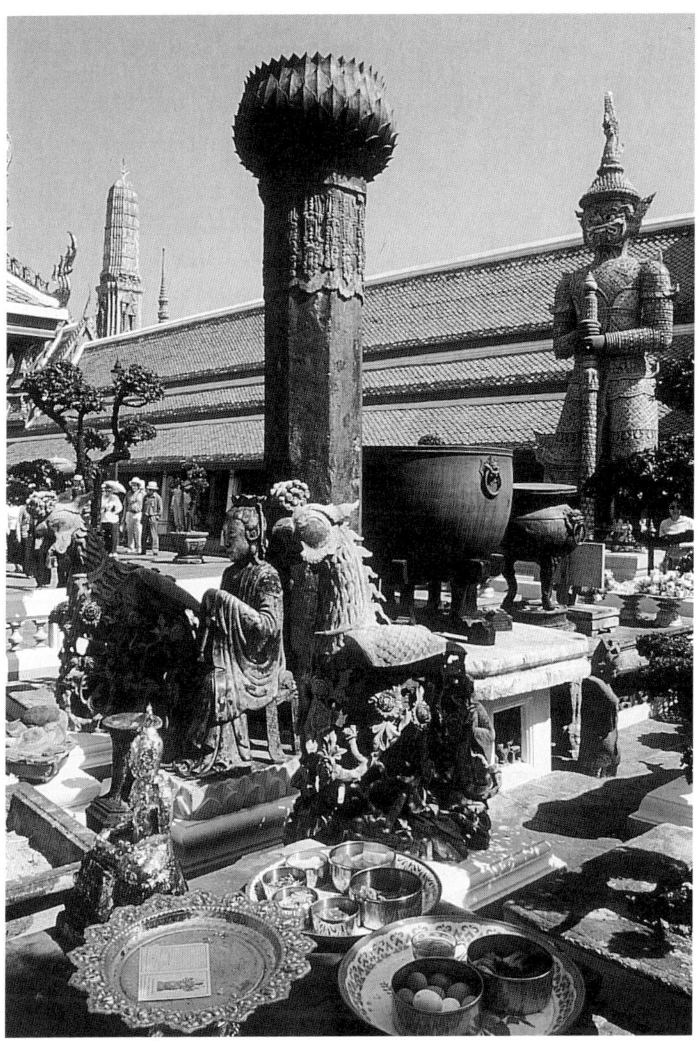

Optimize depth of field in a photograph by using a small aperture and setting focus for the hyperfocal distance.

When this button is pressed, the lens diaphragm closes down to the selected f-stop and the range of what will be in focus can be visually assessed. Using this takes some practice and experience because as the diaphragm closes the image on the viewing screen becomes darker and will be very dark at small apertures and difficult to see. Our recommendation is to practice the use of the depth of field preview button at a variety of lens apertures and in differing lighting conditions to become familiar with its use.

Light Metering System

The Canon EOS-3 has five light-metering modes, each with different metering characteristics and functions: 21-area evaluative (sometimes called matrix), partial, spot, multispot, and center-weighted. With these light-metering modes, you have the whole world of photography in your grasp. In this chapter, we will cover each of these in detail so that you will know which one to use in a variety of photographic situations.

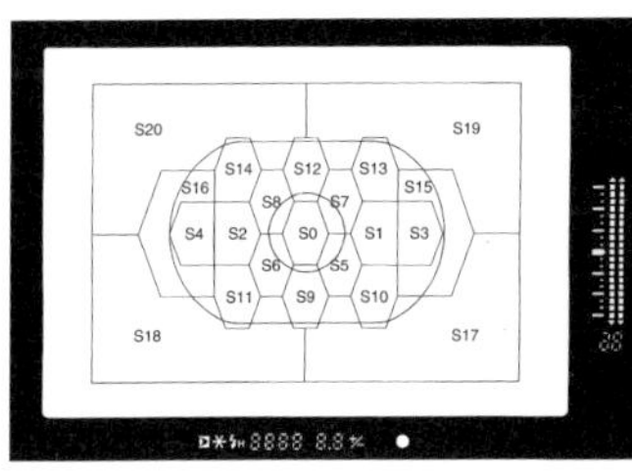

The EOS-3's 21-zone metering pattern.

Even when you're taking photos in rapid sequence—up to seven frames per second with the PB-E2 Power Drive Booster—the EOS-3's super-fast computer and built-in motor drive can still compute each exposure separately, making a separate measurement series before each photo is taken and correcting the exposure if necessary. This is particularly important in sports and wildlife photography, because the subject often moves through areas of different brightness during the sequence of photos.

Evaluative metering will instantly determine the correct exposure standard and professional lighting, even with complex and contrasty subjects. It can also almost always handle difficult subject and light situations, such as strong backlighting, high subject contrast, or subjects that are all of one dark color. There are situations, however, in which the other metering modes will be preferable and help ensure a perfect exposure. In doing so, you will also learn much more about photography, which will prove helpful if you wish to work with special lighting effects.

Evaluative Metering 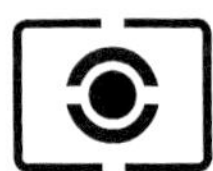

Evaluative metering is activated by pressing the exposure compensation button (the one at the very rear on the left top of the camera) and turning the Main Dial until the appropriate symbol (circle and dot inside rectangle) is displayed on the LCD

This position shows the meter weighted on the far left focusing point.

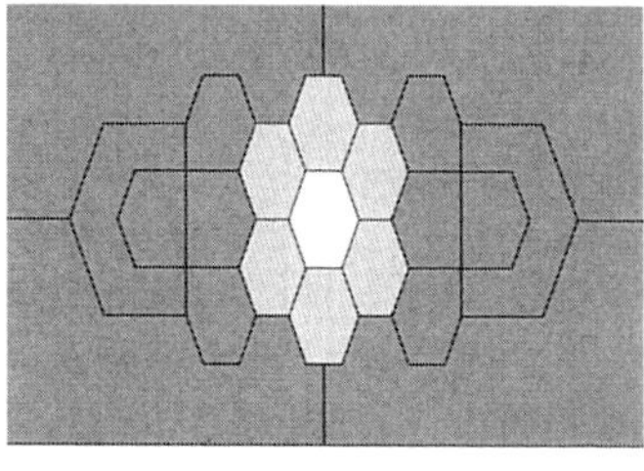

This position shows the meter weighted on the center focusing point.

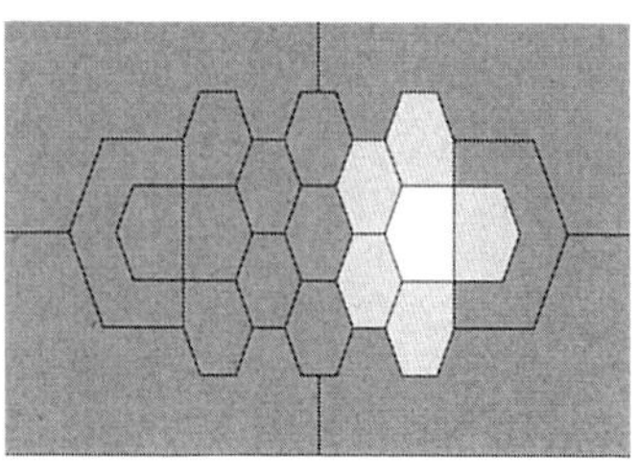

This position shows the meter weighted on the midright focusing point.

panel.When evaluative metering is in use, the entire image area is divided into 21 separate metering areas. So many separate metering areas allows small variations in contrast to be measured and fed to the camera's computer, which then determines subject brightness and contrast based on this information. These metering areas also correspond to the location of specific groups of AF sensors. The camera uses the information from the active AF sensor(s) and puts more weight on that area in determining the overall exposure. So the area on which the camera focuses is also the most important in the exposure determination. In this way, the camera can determine the appropriate exposure for the main subject and then for the background, providing an excellent balance of exposure to favor the main subject. Remember, though, that the exposure reading is taken and stored when you activate the autofocus, so if you set the focus by pressing halfway down on the shutter release button and then recompose the image while retaining pressure on the button, the camera will place exposure emphasis on the light value of the area on which you focused. When you use manual focus, the central metering area is always treated as the area of focus and receives the most weight when exposure is determined.

The symmetrical arrangement of the metering areas and the weighting of metering emphasis on the active AF sensor makes the EOS-3 produce excellent exposures whether held in either the horizontal or vertical orientation. In almost all cases, evaluative metering will provide perfect exposures of a wide variety of lighting conditions, reacting quickly and precisely to changes in lighting, and handling most difficult situations. And, because it places the weight of the exposure on the area on which the camera is focused, it even will handle strongly backlighted subjects automatically. The only problem with all this automation is that the advanced photographer is given no information on just how the exposure was obtained. This makes it very difficult to use the manual exposure compensation when using evaluative metering, because the camera may well have automatically applied the needed compensation. For this reason, the advanced photographer may prefer one of the other metering modes and switch back to evaluative metering primarily for making snapshots. Evaluative metering can be combined with automatic Depth of Field, Program, Aperture Priority, Shutter Priority, and Manual modes.

Partial Metering 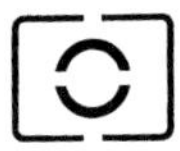

Partial metering is set by pressing the exposure compensation button and turning the Main Dial until the appropriate symbol (empty circle inside rectangle) is displayed on the lower left side of the camera's LCD panel. In this mode, only the five central

Partial metering uses five metering zones in the center, concentrating on 8.5% of the image area.

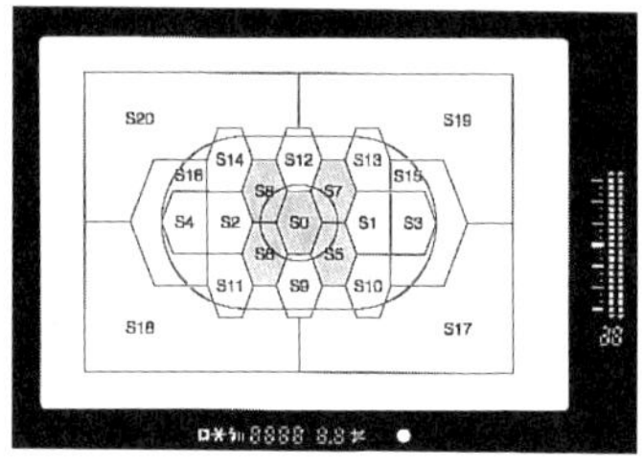

metering areas (the central one and two on each side, left and right) are used and the rest of the 21 metering areas are inactive.

Though the partial metering area is not marked in the viewfinder, it is not hard to envision. Start by visualizing a central circle with a diameter larger than the spot-metering circle but smaller than the upper and lower limits of the AF ellipse, about halfway between the spot metering circle and ellipse. The metering area is about 8.5% of the full area of the image. This 8.5% remains the same regardless of the lens in use, but the angle of coverage of the metering area varies with the focal length of the lens, being wider when a wide-angle lens is used and narrower when a telephoto lens is used.

Partial metering makes possible careful metering of a subject in the center of the viewfinder and is therefore particularly well suited for backlighted subjects. It also works well for subjects in front of very light or very dark backgrounds so long as the subject is not too small to fill the metering area. When used with longer focal length lenses, partial metering allows metering from relatively small areas of a larger subject. When the subject is quite small or the area to be metered is small, however, it makes more sense to use spot metering.

A typical photographic situation for which partial metering is well suited is the subject with strong backlighting. If you wish a more natural look, align the metering area so that a small portion of the backlighting is included to slightly modify the exposure.

Selective area metering may be used with Program, Depth of Field, Shutter Priority, Aperture Priority, and Manual modes.

AE Lock

With the Canon EOS-3, the measured exposure can be locked and held by pressing the AE lock button (marked with an * on the back of the camera). This is conveniently placed to be easily

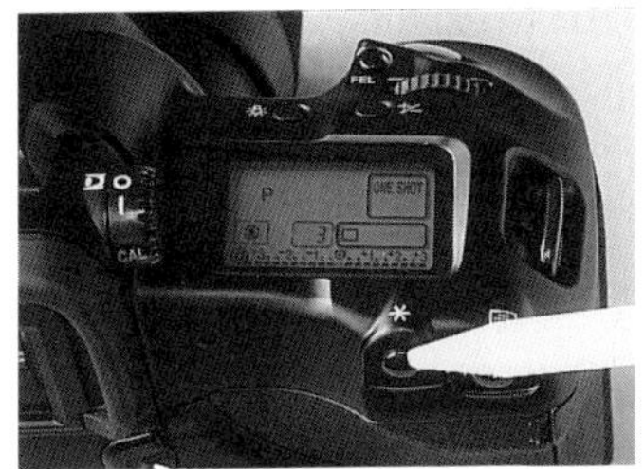

The pointer shows the AE lock button.

reached with the right thumb. Storing and holding the metered light value is particularly useful with partial and spot metering, although it works with the other metering modes as well. When using partial metering, the following method is recommended: Point the central metering area at an area representing the desired metering area. This measured value is then stored by pressing the AE lock button. You can then take your time composing the image exactly as you wish, with full confidence that the exposure value you have stored will be used when you take the photograph. The value remains stored as long as the asterisk is displayed in the viewfinder, which lasts for two seconds after each photo when shooting series photos (motor set for continuous, C), or after six seconds when taking individual photos (motor set for single frame, S). You can cancel the stored value by pressing another button, the most convenient being the metering area selector button just to the right of the AE lock button. Because the metered value is stored immediately when you press the AE lock button, it is extremely important to place the metering area precisely before pressing the button. If the area to be metered from is very small, it is best to switch to spot metering. If you prefer, you can link the AE lock function to the AF function with Custom Function 4, so that pressing halfway on the shutter release button locks both the focus and the exposure.

Spot Metering 

Spot metering is turned on by pressing the exposure compensation button and turning the Main Dial until the symbol of a dot inside a rectangle is displayed on the lower left of the LCD panel. In spot metering, the exposure measurement is made in a very

Spot metering concentrates on a highly selective 2.4% of the image area.

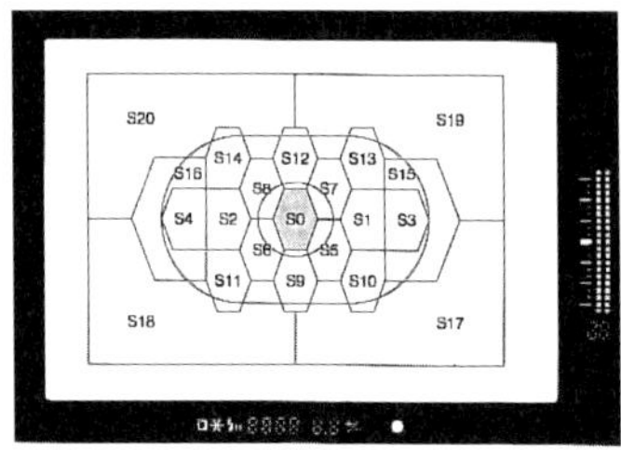

small area, indicated by the small circle in the center of the viewfinder screen. The circle is slightly larger than the actual metering area, which is only 2.4% of the image area; this makes it ideal for metering from very small areas of the subject. Because the 2.4% area does not vary, the actual metering angle changes with the lens in use. This means that you could mount a telephoto lens to take very precise meter readings from small areas and then switch to a wider lens for the actual photo, thus adding very professional spot metering capability to the EOS-3.

Spot metering is best suited for difficult subjects such as relatively small subjects in front of very dark or very light backgrounds, strong backlighting on smaller subjects, and a wide variety of difficult lighting situations. The small measuring area makes it easy to determine contrast ranges of a subject by taking individual meter readings from highlight and shadow areas, although you may find it more convenient to use multispot metering and let the camera do the work for you. The AE lock button works well with spot metering to establish and store exposure information determined from a small area of the subject.

Coupling to AF Sensors

Custom Function 13 allows you to reduce the active AF sensors from 45 to 11 and to couple AF sensors to spot metering, so that the spot meter reading is taken from the area of the active AF sensor. You can choose to select the active sensor by eye control or allow the camera to automatically select it for you. This special setting is recommended for photographing moving subjects in a strong backlighted situation so that the meter reading will always be taken from the subject as it moves to different parts of the image area.

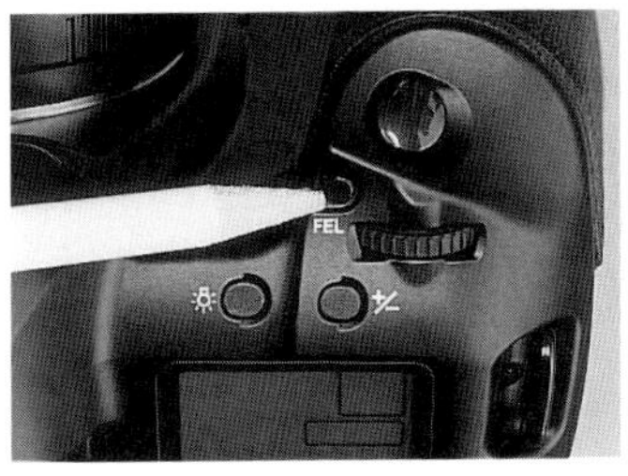

The pointer shows the FEL button.

Multispot Metering

Canon offered multispot metering in a T-90 back in 1986. Many photographers really loved this feature and continually asked Canon to again offer it in an EOS camera. Now the EOS-3 becomes the first member of the EOS family to offer this very professional feature. Basically, multispot metering is a highly refined variant of standard spot metering. Spot meter readings and the camera's computer will use them all to calculate the best possible exposure. This feature is operated by the small button to the left of the shutter release button, marked FEL (Flash Exposure Lock), which is also used in flash photography. To use the multispot metering function, the camera must first be set for standard spot metering. Then the central circle in the viewfinder is placed on the first area to be measured and the FEL button is pressed. The exposure value determined from this single reading is displayed on the scale on the right side inside the viewfinder. The second reading is taken in the same way and an indicator of this exposure value will then appear on the scale. These indicators are displayed to the far right of the scale. Each additional measurement up to the maximum of eight will likewise be displayed by an indicator. The camera will indicate its choice of exposure with a shutter speed and lens aperture combination in the display at the bottom of the viewfinder. A moving indicator on the scale to the right indicates how much the meter reading from the current position of the spot metering circle varies from the stored spot metered values. The maximum time delay between spot readings is 16 seconds. If you do not make another meter reading before this time elapses, the camera shuts down and you must start the procedure once again. The value determined by the camera is stored for up to two seconds when making sequences of photographs.

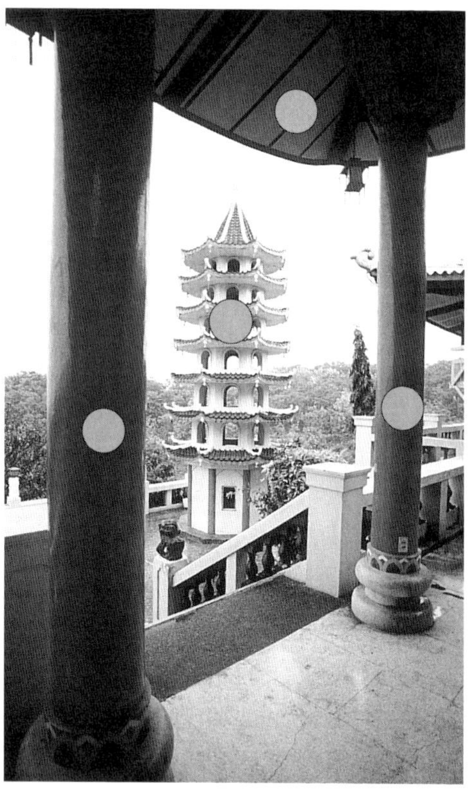

The circles superimposed on this photograph indicate the areas used by the photographer for selective spot metering. By analyzing these readings, the photographer determined the best exposure for the overall scene.

The camera's computer takes all of the stored spot meter values and determines an average exposure based on them, and sets this on the camera automatically. The distance apart on the scale between the highest and lowest readings shows you the contrast range of your subject. This is very important in professional photography, because the photographer knows the maximum contrast range his or her film can record and must ensure that the contrast range of the subject does not exceed this range. The simplest use of multispot metering is to simply take two readings, one from the brightest area that should retain detail and one from the darkest area that also should retain detail. The range between these two readings is a quickly determined contrast range measurement. The metered areas must be selected with care for accurate information. Multispot metering with several measurements represents the next step up. Here you can take two or more readings for shadows and two or more for highlights to fine tune your contrast range measurement. You can further refine this with two or more readings of a midtoned area of your subject. Because the EOS-3 figures out the exposure for you, this method is much simpler than older methods with manual spot meters. It is important, however, to keep in mind the known brightness range your film is capable of dealing with.

The KODAK Gray Card

Another relatively simple but very accurate method of exposure determination can be done by taking a spot meter reading from a KODAK Gray Card, which has an 18% (17.68% precisely) value to work from. This value is the logarithmic average value between pure white (100% reflectance) and pure black (0% reflectance).

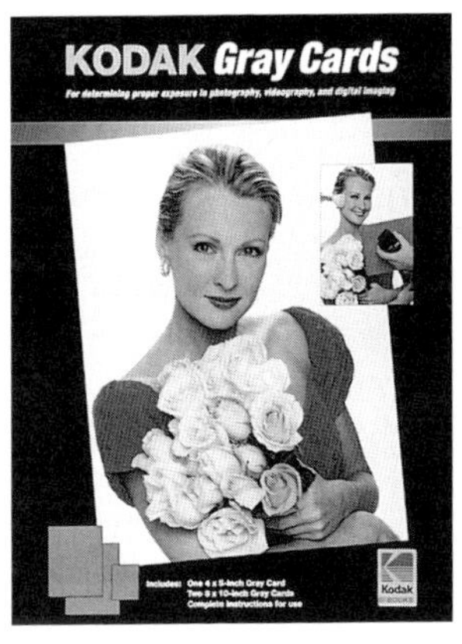

A KODAK Gray Card is a useful exposure aid, particularly with subjects of unusual reflectance or lighting.

Be sure to follow the instructions on the KODAK Gray Card exactly, since very many photographers use them incorrectly. Hold the card vertically and angle it about 1/3 of the angle between the lens axis and the main light source. Modify this base reading by opening the lens aperture by 1/2 stop or slowing the shutter by 1/2 stop (in default, the Canon EOS-3 only allows settings in 1/3 values, but compensation by 1/3 should be accurate enough for most situations). The reason for making this adjustment is that light meters are calibrated to assume a reflectance of 12%-13%, or 1/2 stop brighter than 18% reflectance. See also page 78 for more on the KODAK Gray Card.

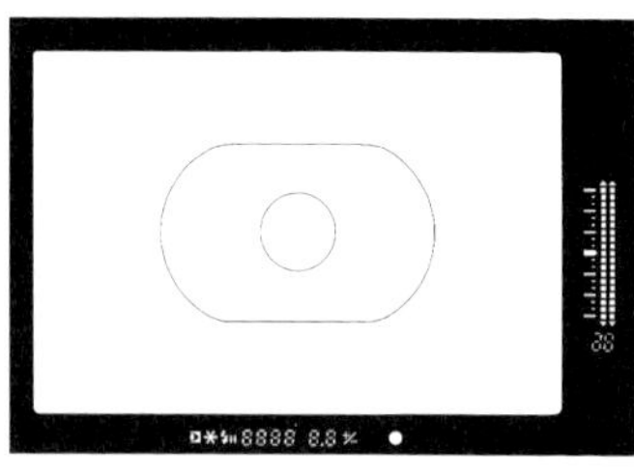

Center-weighted metering is weighted at the center and then averaged for the entire picture.

Center-Weighted Averaging Metering 

This is one of the earliest forms of light metering designed for SLR cameras and is somewhat of an anachronism in a modern camera today. But many serious amateur and professional photographers learned photography using cameras with this metering mode and have grown accustomed to it, so Canon offers it as an option. This mode is accessed as the other metering modes are—by pressing the exposure compensation button and turning the Main Dial until the appropriate symbol, in this case an empty rectangle, is displayed in the lower left of the camera's LCD panel

In this mode, the metering system measures the entire image area but puts more weight on the readings from the center of the image. The area receiving this extra emphasis is slightly smaller than the AF ellipse in the viewfinder.

Center-weighted metering is well suited only to subjects of average brightness and contrast. In almost all situations, evaluative metering will produce superior results, and we recommend center-weighted average metering only to experienced photographers who are already familiar with it. Because it does no automatic compensation of any sort, some photographers may prefer to use center-weighted averaging metering because they then know exactly what it is doing and can apply exposure compensation or manual correction when they know it will be needed. We do not recommend this metering mode for beginners.

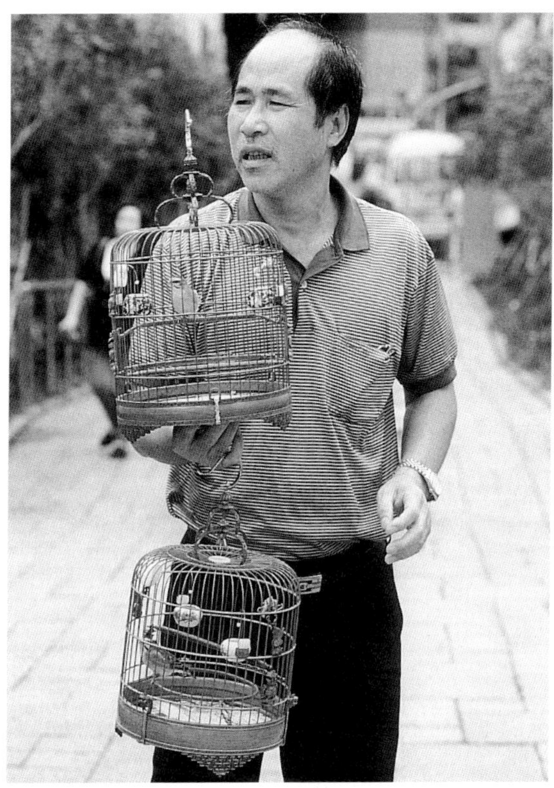

This casual street portrait was shot using autofocus with evaluative metering.

Summary of Metering Modes

Autofocus-coupled evaluative metering is the easiest of the metering modes to use and will work well for the vast majority of subjects and lighting conditions. When photographing subjects with very high contrast, however, you cannot always rely on this mode to determine the exposure with absolute accuracy. Back-lighting, depending on how strong and the type and contrast of the subject, can also sometimes fool this very smart camera when you're using evaluative metering. Because you are unaware of any corrections made by the camera, you cannot rely on exposure compensation to solve the problems of these situations. Therefore, one of the other metering modes may be better suited to certain difficult subjects.

Partial metering and spot metering are often better suited to the advanced photographer, who wants the perfect exposure of difficult subjects and lighting.

Multispot metering allows the precise measurement of the contrast range of the subject. It is ideal for very deliberate workers who want the best out of their film.

Center-weighted averaging metering is suited only for subjects with no difficulties—subjects with average brightness in average lighting. It is particularly recommended for experienced photographers who are already accustomed to using it.

Bulb (Time Exposure) Setting

There are subjects and situations that cannot be measured by any light metering system with precision. Examples are fireworks displays and thunderstorms. In these situations, the only thing that works in empirical information and/or experience. In the two examples just cited you would use the Bulb (time exposure) setting and manual focus. Activate the Bulb setting by pressing the mode button and turning the Main Dial until you see [buLb] on the LCD panel. When set this way, the camera shutter will remain open as long as pressure is maintained on the shutter release button. This may be easier to do with a remote release cable. It is also best to use a sturdy stand or tripod for this sort of photography. Because you will be unable to look through the viewfinder during the exposure, you must guess where the fireworks or lightning will be and set the camera up accordingly. Due to its greater exposure latitude, it is best to use negative film. A good starting point is to set

Top: Depth of field is minimized by a short focusing distance. To maximize sharpness of all of the elements in the still life composition, the photographer focused on an object in the middle of the grouping. ➪

Bottom: In the composition, the photographer chose a large aperture so that the cigar boxes would appear unsharp. This provided a soft, pleasant backdrop for the image.

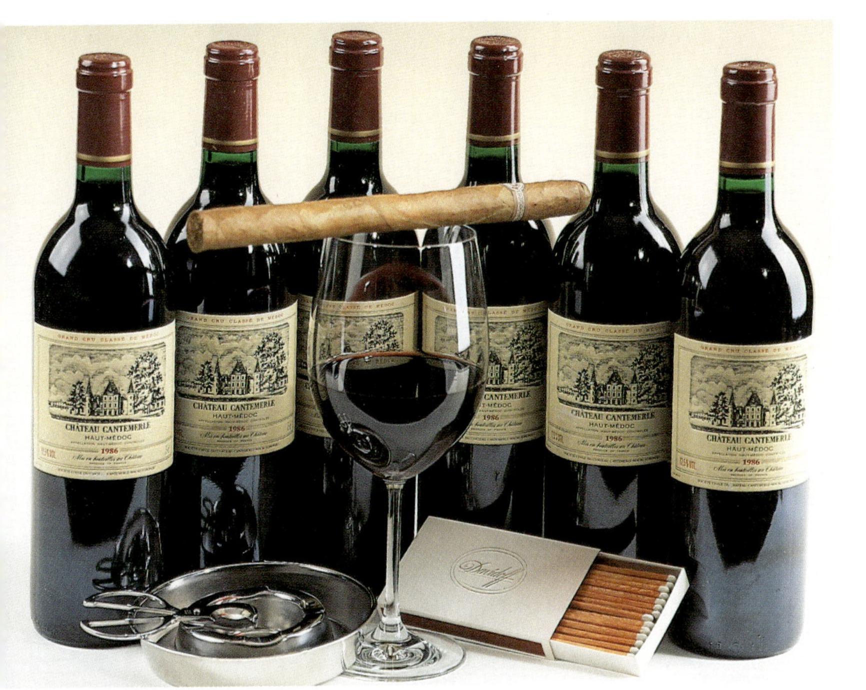

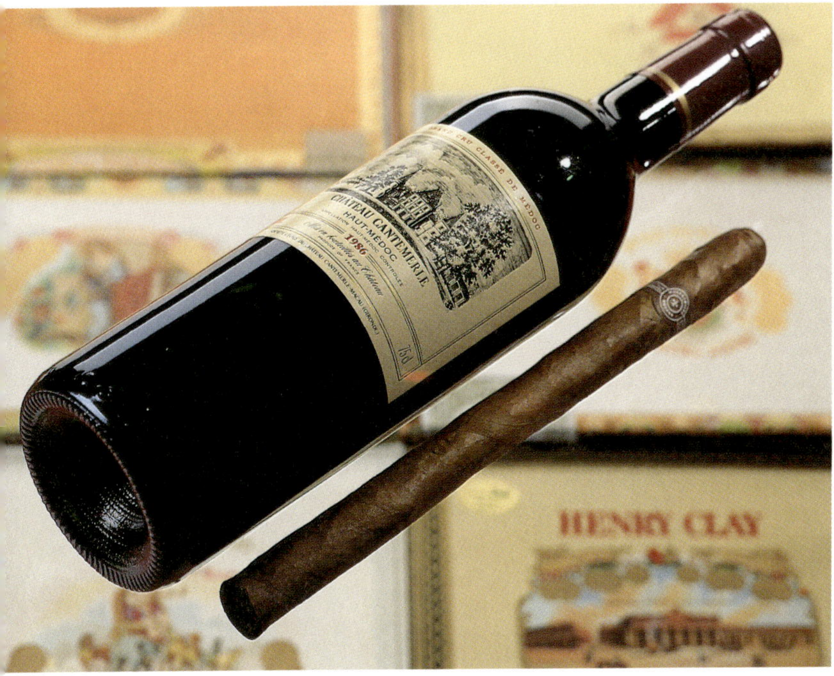

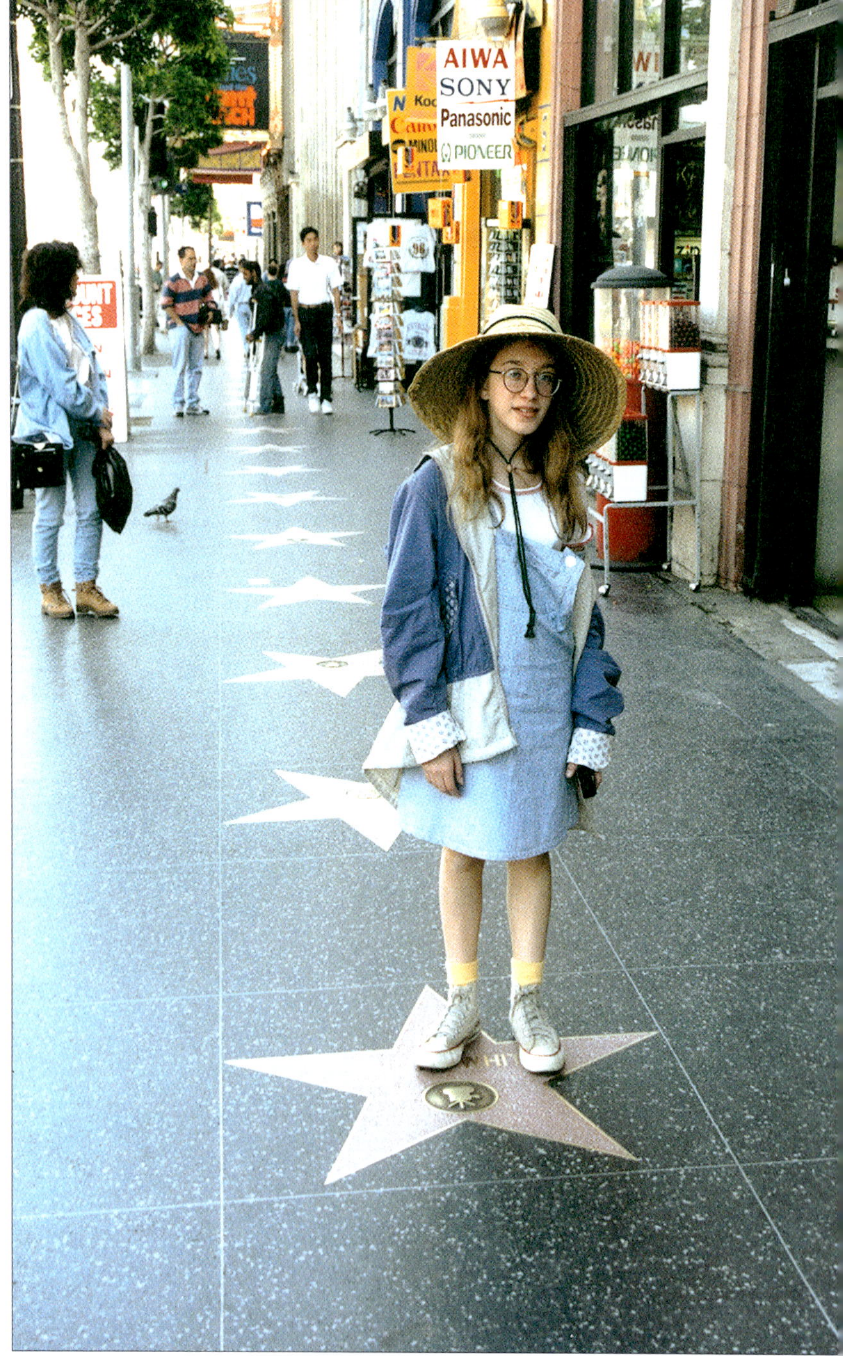
AIWA
SONY
Panasonic
PIONEER

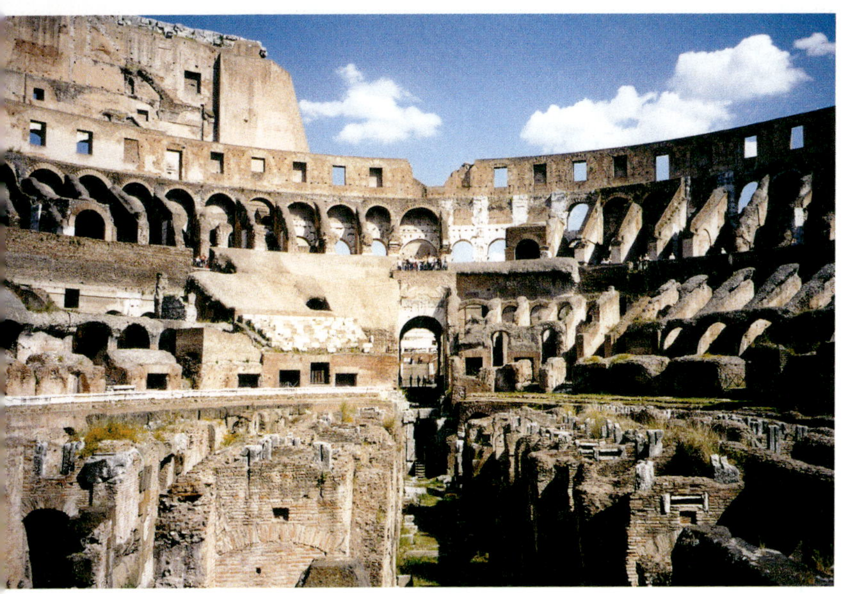

Above: The photographer took advantage of Depth of Field mode for this shot of the Colosseum, in Rome. This sophisticated mode selects the proper aperture for maintaining acceptable sharpness throughout the scene. Photo by Rebecca Saltzman.

Left: Contrary to most rules of portraiture, when making an environmental portrait it is best to use a small aperture, because that lets the background, which remains sharp, tell the story. Photo by Rebecca Saltzman.

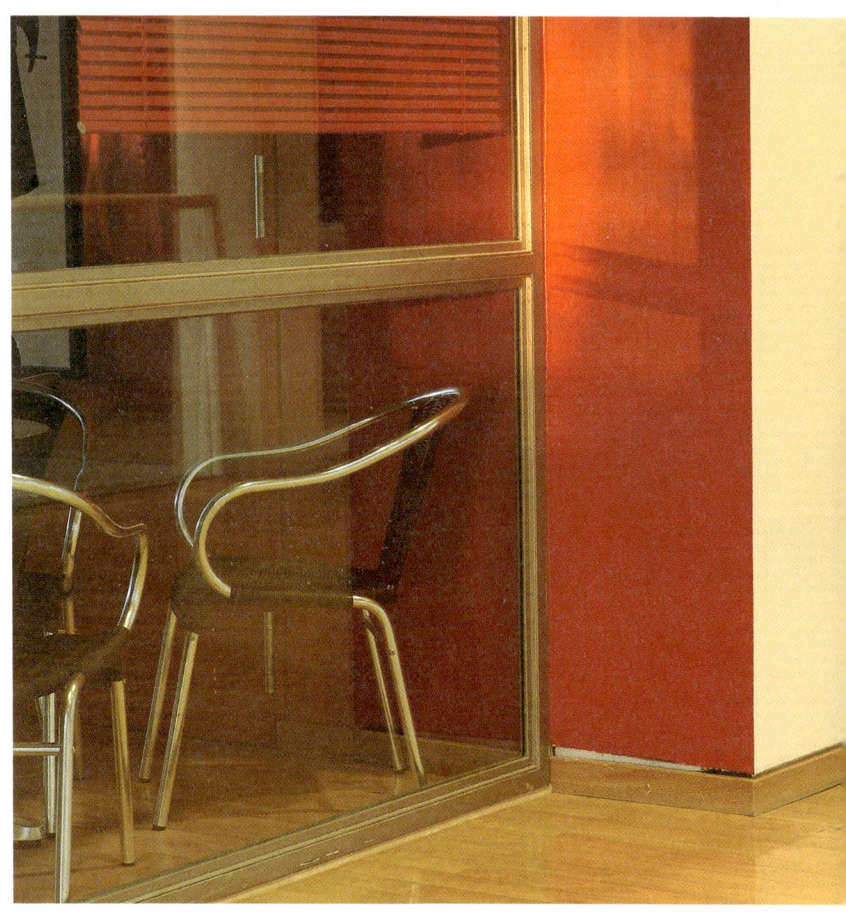

Above: This architectural study was shot using the Ec-D focusing screen, which is etched with a grid. The grid helps to prevent parallax distortion when photographing buildings.

Top right: The blend of natural and artificial light that was present in this scene gave a pleasing ambiance to this study in interior photography.

Bottom right: A Tiffen® star filter was used to take this picture of candles in Notre Dame cathedral, in Paris. Photograph by Rebecca Saltzman.

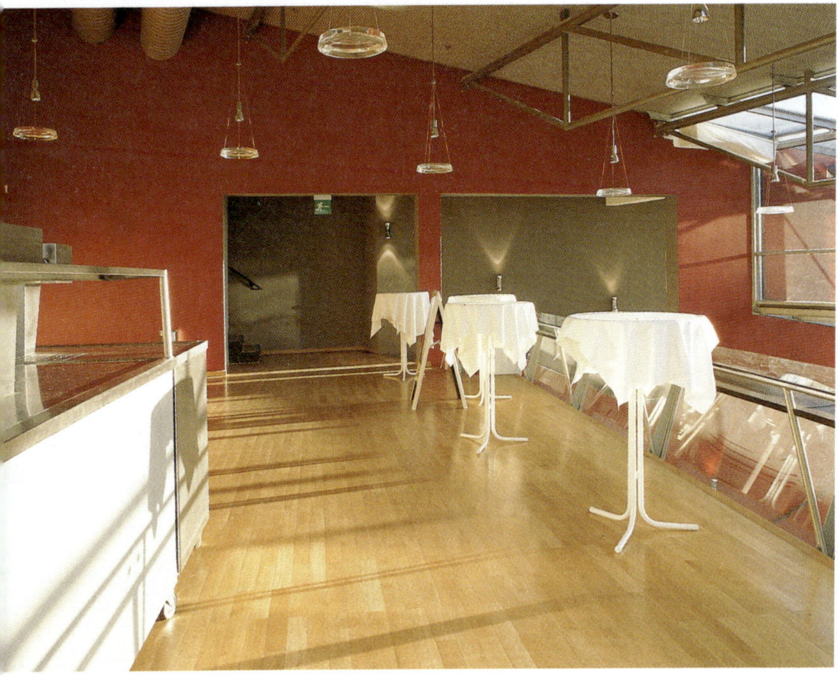

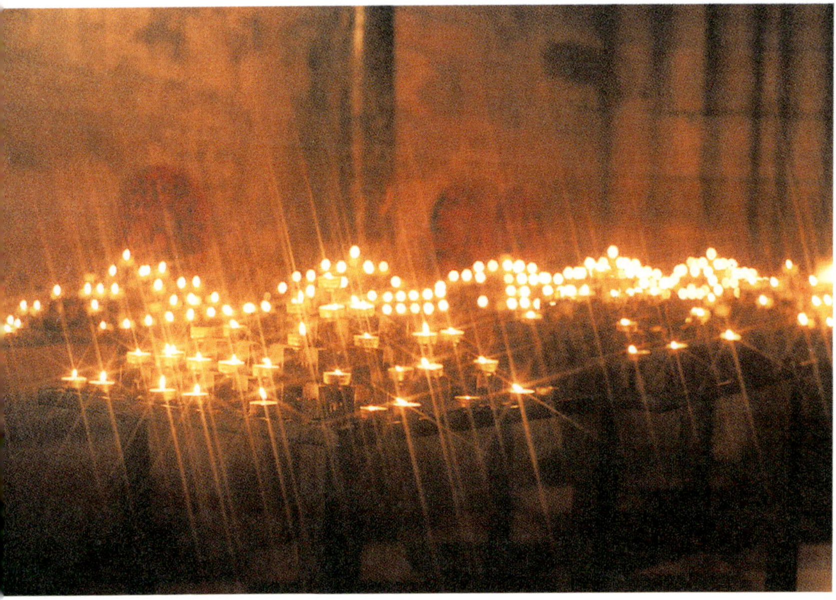

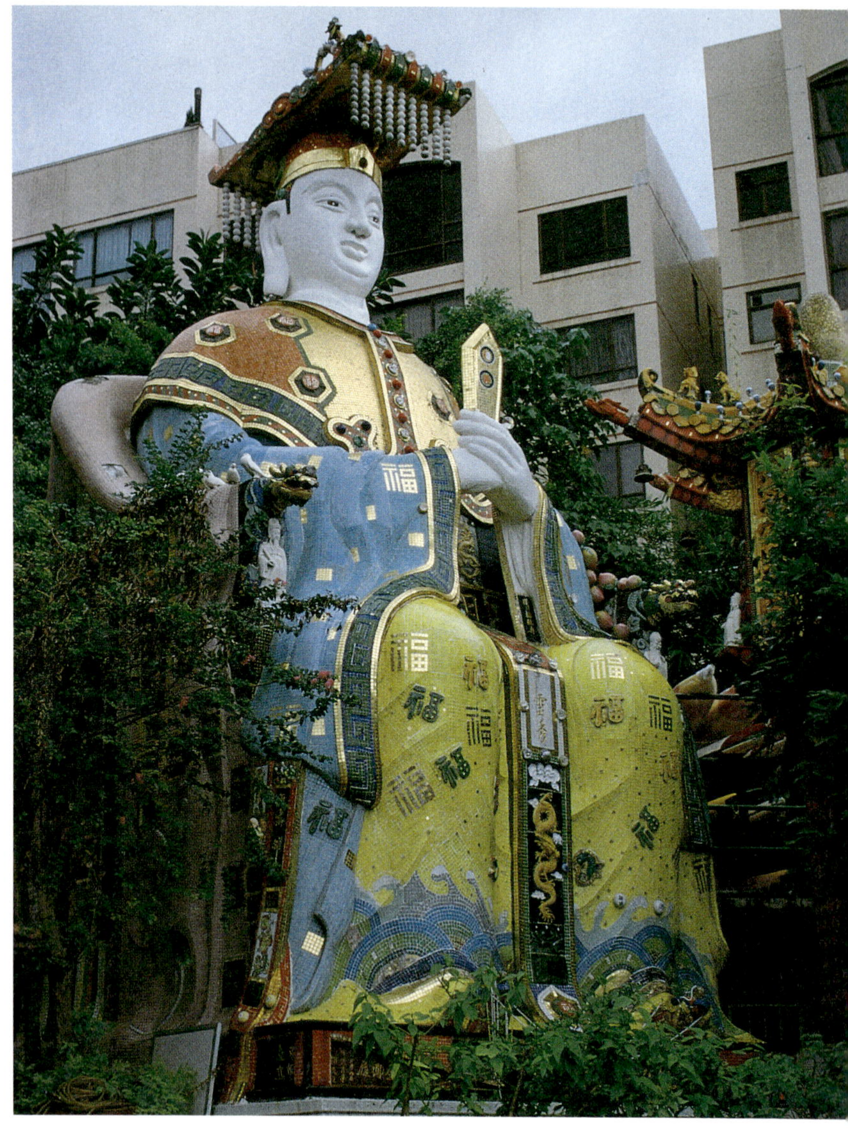

Above: Evenly illuminated subjects, as in the travel picture above, are best shot using Program mode and autofocus.

On the right: This classic composition employs the rule of thirds.

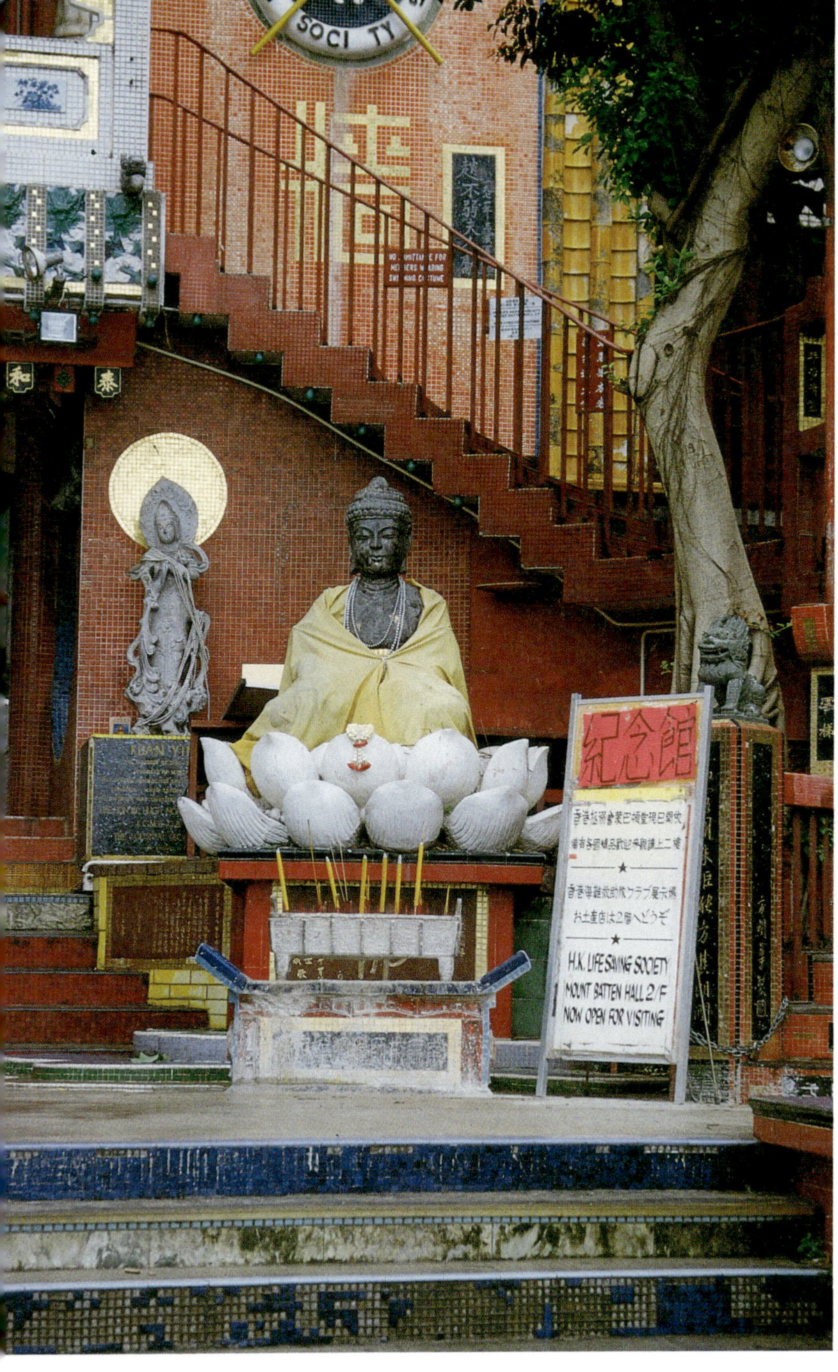
SOCI TY
和
泰
紀念館
お土産店は2階へどうぞ
H.K. LIFE SAVING SOCIETY
MOUNT BATTEN HALL 2/F
NOW OPEN FOR VISITING

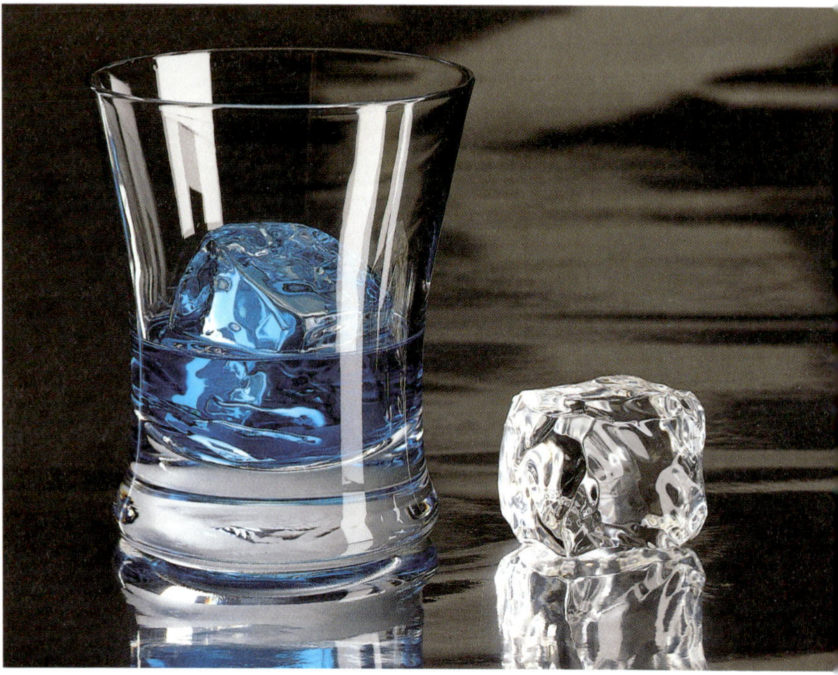

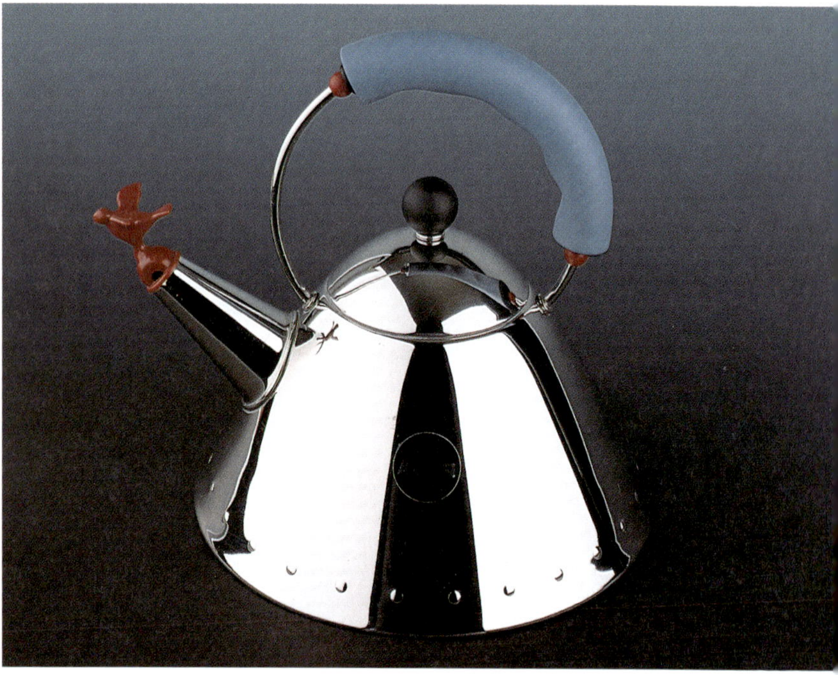

the lens diaphragm for f/8 with ISO 100 film and experiment with exposure times from five to 30 seconds to get multiple fireworks or multiple lightning flashes on one frame of film. Please remember that lightning is very dangerous, so observe all possible precautions when attempting to photograph thunderstorms. See page 93 for more discussion of Bulb mode.

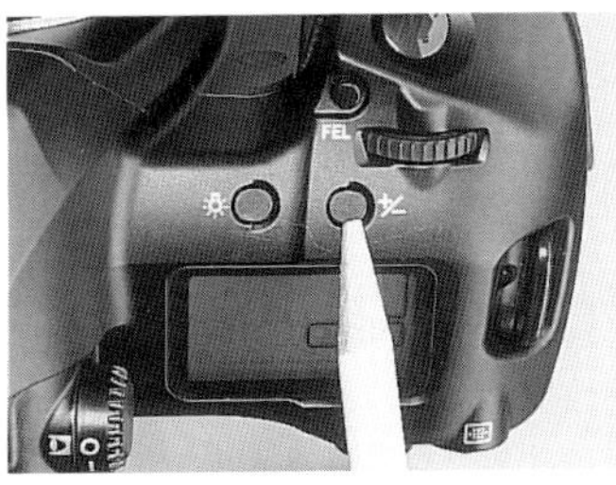

The pointer shows the exposure compensation button.

Exposure Compensation

Exposure compensation is a very important camera function because it allows you to intentionally alter the exposure control of the camera without the inconvenience of switching to Manual mode.

With the Canon EOS-3, you have two possible ways to input exposure compensation. The most direct way is to press the exposure compensation button (just behind the Main Dial and marked with +/–) and use the Main Dial to dial in the amount of compensation you want, or, after pressing the shutter release halfway to activate the meter, you can input exposure compensation with the Quick Control Dial. Just remember that the Quick Control Dial is turned on and off by the switch just above it and does nothing when turned off. Leaving the Quick Control Dial switched off except when actually using it can avoid accidental input of exposure compensation. The camera stores and holds the exposure compensation you have dialed in until you manually return the setting to 0.

Product shots of highly reflective objects such as these require that the photographer have a sophisticated knowledge of studio lighting equipment.

The exposure compensation you have set is indicated on a bar scale along the bottom of the LCD and by a +/– symbol in the viewfinder, as well as an indicator mark on the exposure scale seen at far right in the viewfinder. Compensation can be entered up to three stops in 1/3-stop increments, either plus or minus. If you wish to use half-stop increments instead, you can change this with Custom Function 6. Exposure compensation can be used in any exposure mode, but really does not make much sense in spot and multispot metering. Experienced photographers may find it necessary to input exposure compensation to get the results that they want, particularly when using center-weighted metering. Using exposure compensation in evaluative metering is not advised, because you do not know what compensation the camera may have already applied.

Even the most sophisticated metering system such as in the Canon EOS-3 has its limitations, however. This is why you may get better photographs of subjects with extremely high contrast or very strong backlighting by dialing in an exposure compensation. At the beach, in the snow, or in any situation in which the light is very bright and glare tends to be high your camera may be fooled into underexposing the photos, which will render bright areas as gray. In such cases, you may wish to experiment by setting exposure compensation of +2/3, or even more. When trying this for the first time, always take the photo without compensation first and then with the compensation so you can accurately judge the results when your film comes back. Similarly, when photographing very dark subjects against dark backgrounds you may need to do the reverse and dial in a minus exposure compensation.

Automatic Bracketing

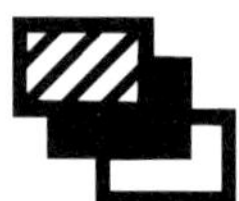

The professional photographer's motto used to be "When in doubt, bracket." Bracketing means to take one photograph at the light meter's recommended settings and then take a series of exposures on both sides around that setting. This had been complicated to do, but many modern cameras, including the EOS-3, have automated the procedure.

The Canon EOS-3 automatic bracketing feature is turned on by pressing the mode and the AF mode buttons at the same time

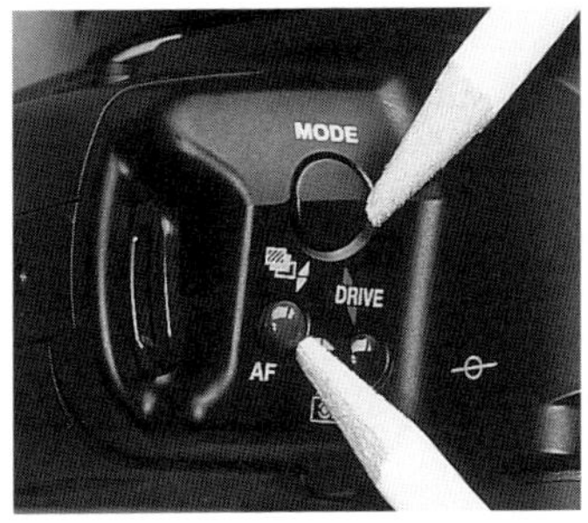

The pointers show the mode and AF mode buttons, which are used to initiate automatic bracketing.

and then using the Main Dial to dial in the desired amount of exposure bracketing. Just as with the exposure compensation, this is indicated on the graph at the bottom of the LCD panel and in the graph in the viewfinder. This time, three index marks are used, one for the exposure determined by the camera's metering system and one each for the under- and overexposure brackets. The brackets can be set in 1/3-stop increments, but can be switched to half-stop increments with Custom Function 6.

Automatic bracketing can be used with exposure compensation to shift the entire bracketed sequence toward over- or underexposure. Also, you can use single-frame or continuous motor settings with automatic bracketing. When set for continuous motor operation, the camera takes three bracketed exposures in rapid succession each time the shutter release button is pressed. With single-frame advance, each photo in the bracketed series is taken separately.

In general, it makes little sense to bracket in values smaller than +1 and –1 with color negative or black-and-white negative film because their exposure latitude is so great. Reserve the 1/3-stop brackets for slide (transparency) film. In the default settings, the camera takes the normal exposure first, followed by the bracketed exposures.

Bracketed photos can be taken in Aperture Priority (Av) mode, in which bracketing will be done by altering shutter speed. In Shutter Priority (Tv) mode, the bracketing is done by varying the aperture. In Program (P) mode, exposure compensation follows a program of its own.

Using bracketed exposures is highly recommended, particularly with slide film, when you are confronted with subjects and situation that are "one time only." After all, film is still the cheap-

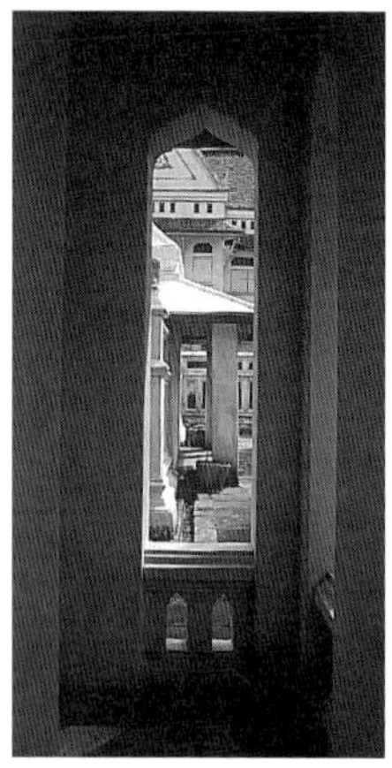
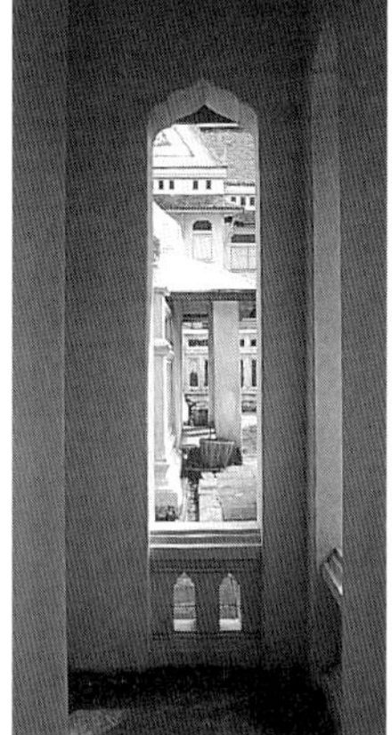
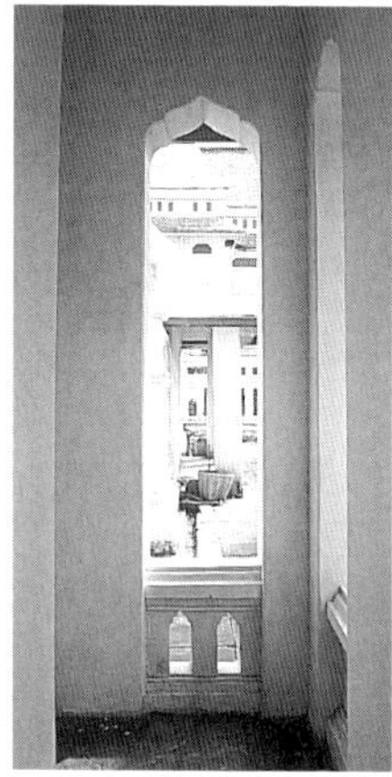

Automatic bracketing was used in this series to determine the best exposure to make the most of this difficult-to-meter spot.

est part of photography, and it does no harm to dedicate some frames to ensure getting the perfect photo.

High-Key Photographs

High-key photographs generally consist of very bright colors and often lots of white. They can be very impressionistic and capture a special atmosphere. Bright subjects in front of bright backgrounds that are nearly shadowless are good subjects for high-key photographs. Intentionally dialing in an exposure compensation of +1 or even +2 can accentuate the effect.

Low-Key Photographs

Essentially, low-key photographs are simply the opposite of high-key ones and require dealing with them in reverse. These photos consist of large areas of dark colors or heavy shadows. Portraits, still lifes, nudes, and many other subjects are often photographed in low key. Dialing in an exposure compensation of –1 or –2 can work well, depending on the subject and the desired look of the photograph. Small highlights or light areas can accentuate the look of a low-key image.

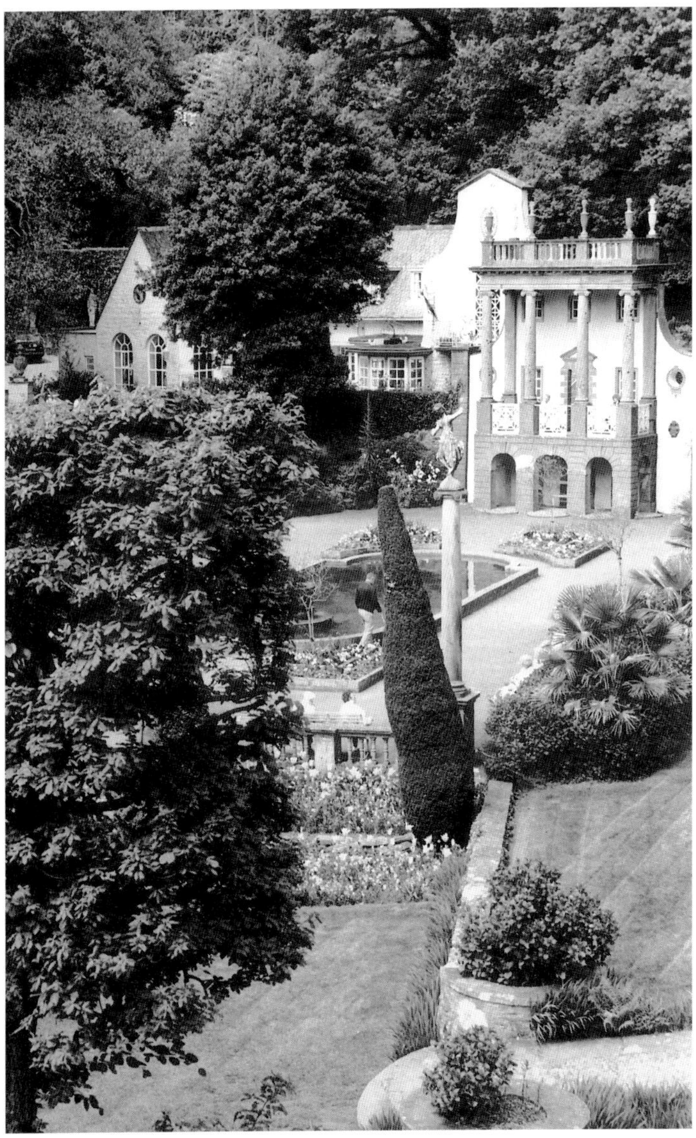

Don't underestimate black-and-white film for travel photography. Monotone photos have drama and interest, and look great, nicely framed, on a wall. Photo by Bob Shell.

Exposure Metering

The AF-coupled evaluative metering system of the Canon EOS-3 is an excellent metering system that can handle the majority of exposure situations and subjects with no problems. Center-weighted and partial metering can also be useful to some photographers. Spot and multispot metering can be invaluable in difficult situations. But just how do you know when to use each one?

You must be familiar with the functions of an exposure meter. It makes no difference whether you are using the camera's built-in metering system or a separate hand light meter, the principles are the same. Today's cameras use TTL (through-the-lens) metering. This means that the exposure is measured through the lens, which actually takes the photograph. This method has many advantages, but also disadvantages—particularly that the metering system is calibrated to a medium gray tone and will therefore set the exposure to render a white handkerchief or a black felt hat as medium gray. It is very important to keep this in mind any time you are using a light meter, which measures light reflected from the subject. The meter always will "assume" that the subject is medium gray in color and set exposure accordingly. This is the reason that most professional photographers carry a KODAK Gray Card (see page 61) in their camera bag. Because the card is a neutral gray subject of known reflectance, it is helpful to use when photographing subjects of very light or very dark color, or in very bright or very dark illumination. Taking a meter reading from the card is preferred to produce an accurate exposure.

Often you cannot use a KODAK Gray Card because it is impossible to get it into the light falling on your subject. You can memorize some readily available standards, then, and meter accordingly. As an example, green grass in summer reflects about a half stop less than a photographic midtone. Thus, you would add a manual compensation of –0.5 to the meter reading taken from a field of grass. If you cannot get close enough to fill the frame with the grass, switch to the spot meter. If the area still is not large enough to fill the spot metering circle in the viewfinder, zoom in or use a telephoto lens to make the reading.

Another example of a problem photo is a landscape photographed with a wide-angle lens and including a very large area of bright sky. If you understand that that the large area of sky can cause your camera to underexpose the whole photo, then you can correct for this by inputting a plus exposure compensation. Alternately, you can take an exposure reading with your camera meter and set the camera manually. Just do not forget to add the +0.5-stop correction to compensate for the fact that 18% is one half stop brighter than a photographic midtone (12%-13%).

The evaluative metering of the Canon EOS-3 does an exceptional job with almost any subject and lighting situation. In most cases, you can just let it do its job while you concentrate on composition. Just remember that even this highly sophisticated meter can be fooled by subjects that are overall very light or very dark.

Contrast Range and Exposure Range

The contrast range of a film is the difference between the brightest area that produces detail and the darkest area that produces detail on the film. In the developed negative or transparency, the range is called the density range of the film, and varies with the specific type of film. If you draw this on a graph, you get a sloping line with a rounded "toe" at the bottom and a rounded "shoulder" at the top. Proper exposure places the subject values largely on the straight part of the curve, avoiding the shoulder and toe for critical areas. This is what you are doing with multi-spot metering and what the camera does for you in evaluative metering. Generally speaking, negative films have a longer straight-line area, making them easier to work with.

When encountering a subject with too much contrast to render well on film, you have some options. You can use a color negative film with very great exposure latitude, you can use black-and-white film and alter the development to increase the exposure range, or you can change the contrast range of the subject by throwing light into the shadows with reflectors or with electronic flash. Canon's electronic flash units, often called fill flash or syncro sunlight, are exceptionally good for this purpose. E-TTL metering—which uses the camera's evaluative metering in combination with Canon's Advanced Integrated Multipoint (AIM) system to read through the lens but not off the film—is a Canon innovation available only when using Canon Speedlite EX flash unit cameras.

Subject contrast is easily determined with the EOS-3 in multi-spot metering, perhaps using a long lens to more narrowly define the areas that the spot meter readings are taken from. First, take a spot meter reading from the brightest subject area that should retain detail; then, repeat this procedure with the darkest area that should retain detail. You can do this in the reverse order as well. The contrast range is then clearly visible on the graph scale on the LCD panel and inside the viewfinder.

Exposure Modes

The Canon EOS-3 offers Program, Depth of Field, Shutter Priority, Aperture Priority, Manual, and Bulb (Time) exposure modes. These modes can be used in conjunction with other camera functions, including evaluative, center-weighted-averaging, or spot metering, single or continuous motor drive, and AF modes. It is possible to set each exposure mode to perfectly capture the image the photographer wishes: separating a subject from a confusing background, depicting a landscape with great depth of field, capturing sports in motion, or taking quick snapshots in rapidly changing conditions.

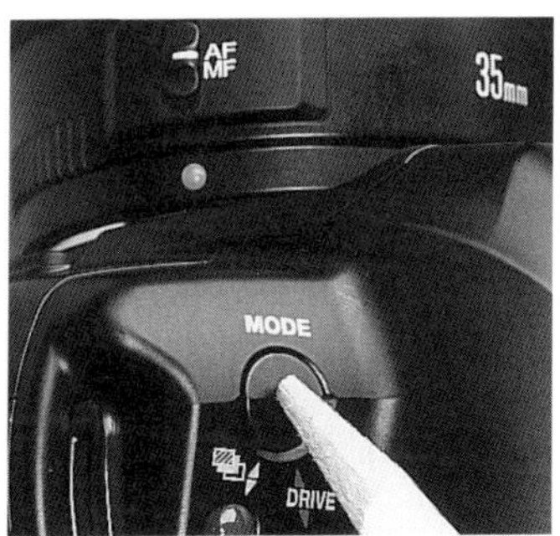

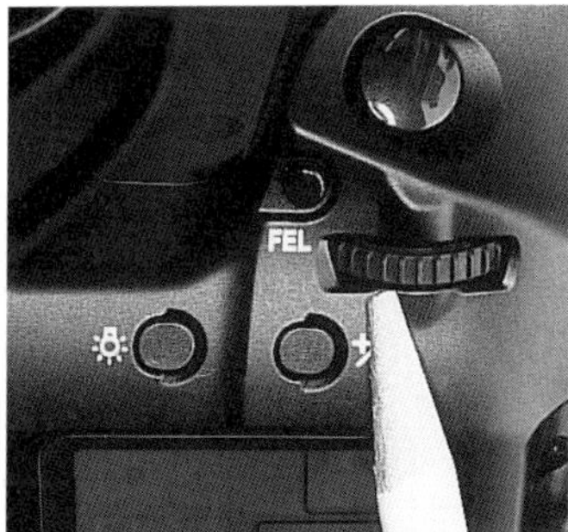

Program mode is accessed by pressing the mode button and turning the Main Dial.

Program Mode

Program mode (shiftable) is an extremely flexible exposure mode that can be used for most subjects and situations. It is set by pressing the mode button and turning the Main Dial until [P] appears on the camera's LCD panel.

In this mode, in normal situations, the camera's computer chooses an appropriate combination of lens aperture and shutter speed based on light levels and the focal length of the lens in use.

But this mode can also be changed (or "shifted") to better fit a specific exposure situation. Program shift allows you to quickly and easily alter the shutter speed and aperture to make the photograph more closely match your conception. That could mean a smaller lens aperture for greater depth of field, or it could mean a faster shutter speed to freeze action, or the reverse; in any case, the relationship between shutter speed and aperture will be maintained so that an accurate exposure is provided. Program shift can be combined with exposure compensation. The shift in Program mode offers all of the advantages of shutter priority and aperture priority without the necessity of learning about those modes in detail.

To use the shift, press down halfway on the shutter release button and turn the Main Dial. As you turn the dial, you will see both the shutter speed and lens aperture values changing in the viewfinder display. You can easily change to a larger or smaller aperture value or faster or slower shutter speed, and the camera will retain the memorized exposure value (EV) to maintain proper exposure.

After you make an exposure, you must maintain half pressure on the shutter release button to retain the shift. The shift is maintained as long as the LCD panel in the viewfinder is illuminated, so if you wish to take a rapid succession of photos with the same shift, do not allow the viewfinder display to turn off. If it does turn off, you must reset the shift by once again pressing halfway on the shutter release button and turning the Main Dial. Program shift does not work if you have a Canon-dedicated flash in the hot shoe and it is turned on.

In Program mode of the Canon EOS-3, all functions are open to you to use: TTL flash operation, different AF modes, and different motor drive speeds, as well as exposure compensation and auto exposure bracketing, self-timer, and other camera functions. As the basic settings for general photography, we recommend evaluative metering, one-shot autofocus, and automatic AF area selection. This settings are ideal for the beginner who has yet to learn the more professional features of this camera.

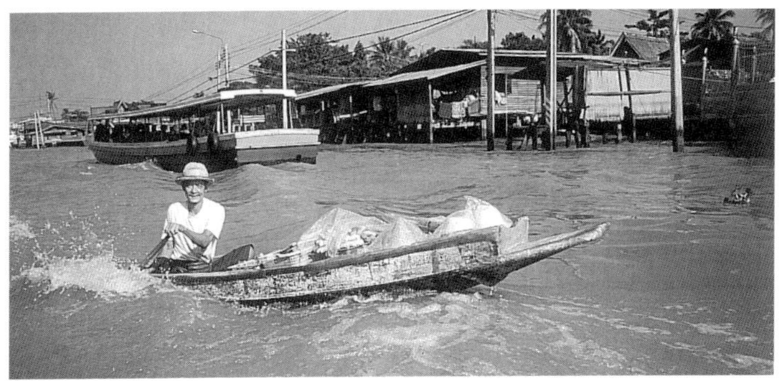

Program mode is ideal for travel snapshots taken on bright sunny days.

Snapshots

Snapshots—spontaneous, natural-looking pictures—are often more interesting than posed or planned photos. Snapshots are not just for the beginner. They can capture the memory of a happy time or hold an impressive moment. It is not always possible to anticipate when the best opportunity to take a snapshot will occur, as action in uncontrolled situations can't be predicted. For this reason, Program mode makes the EOS-3 ideal for snapshot photography.

Depth of Field Mode

What Is Depth of Field?

Depth of field is the area between the nearest and furthest points from the camera that are acceptably sharp in an image; following a law of optics, it appears to be distributed about 1/3 in front of the plane of focus and about 2/3 behind it. When any three-dimensional object is photographed, only one subject plane can be rendered in sharpest focus. In front of and in back of this plane of sharpness, each point on the subject is rendered as a circle. The farther from the plane of sharpness, the larger the circle. When we look at an image, we perceive these circles as sharp points so long as they are smaller than a certain size due to the limits of our visual resolution, and this gives the impression of a zone of sharpness on both sides of the actual plane of focus. The largest circle, which will appear as a sharp point, is called the "circle of least confusion." Smaller diaphragm openings produce smaller circles, and this is what gives the impression of greater depth of field at smaller diaphragm openings. Thus, there can be no absolute definition of depth of field because the size of the circle of least confusion depends on the size of the final image and the viewing distance from that image. Depth-of-field tables have been developed from photographers' experience and practice to give what size circle of least confusion will produce a sharp-looking area.

This diagram illustrates the principle behind Depth of Field mode.

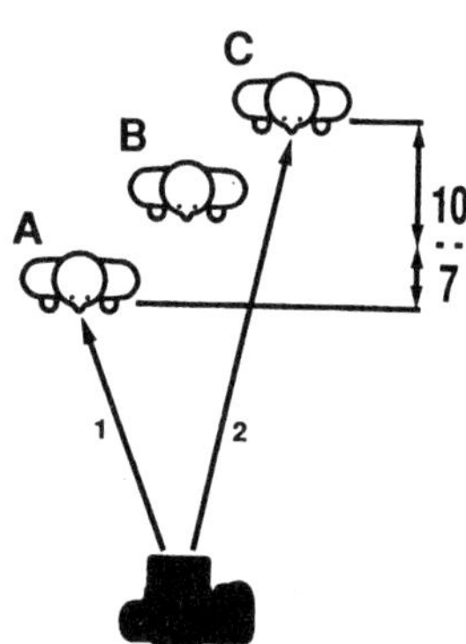

Using Depth of Field Mode

Canon is the only camera maker to offer this unique exposure mode. Depth of Field (DEP) mode functions only with autofocus, so make sure your lens is set for AF operation before you attempt to use this mode. When the camera is set for automatic selection of the AF sensor, only the central sensor is active in DEP mode.

To activate DEP mode, press the mode button and turn the Main Dial until [DEP] is displayed on the LCD panel. To use DEP mode, first, press halfway on the shutter release button with a subject at the closest desired distance of the depth of field until [dEP 1] appears in the viewfinder display and the in-focus indicator appears. Then depress the shutter release button all the way to lock and store this distance. Press the shutter release button halfway again and [dEP 2] will appear in the LCD. Lock in the far limit of your desired depth of field by pressing the shutter release button all the way again. Now recompose the photo and press halfway on the shutter release button again to see the lens aperture and shutter speed the camera has selected. Often, when you are seeking great depth of field, this will be a slow shutter speed, so it is often necessary to use the camera on a tripod in this mode. It is of no importance whether you measure the nearest limit first and the farthest second, or if you reverse the procedure—DEP mode will work either way.

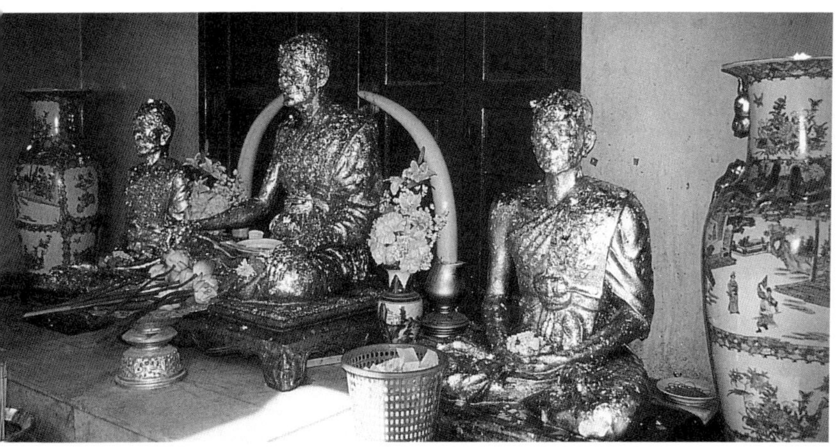

By locking on two focusing points—the vase on the right and the statue on the left—the photographer used Depth of Field mode to produce clear focus throughout this picture.

You can also use DEP mode to limit depth of field by taking both depth-of-field measurements at the same or nearly the same distance. This can be useful when you wish to isolate a subject from a distracting background by putting the background out of focus.

In either case, if it is impossible to provide the depth of field you desire with the lens you have mounted, the aperture-setting indicator in the viewfinder and on the LCD panel will flash as a warning; you can then decide on a different depth of field or switch to a different lens. To cancel DEP mode without taking a photo, just press the mode button and switch to a different mode for a moment and then switch back to DEP.

In DEP mode, the exposure measurement is made just before the exposure. It is technically possible to use DEP mode with on-camera flash, but doing so defeats the purpose of this mode. When using a zoom lens, do not change the zoom position when making the dEP 1 and dEP 2 settings.

Depth of field is governed by other factors besides the aperture size. It is also larger when subject magnification is smaller (as with a wide-angle lens used at a distance), or smaller when subject magnification is greater (as with a telephoto lens used up close).

If subject magnification is exactly the same, depth of field will be exactly the same at any given lens aperture, regardless of the focal length of the lens.

For more on depth of field, see page 50.

Shutter Priority (Tv) Automatic Exposure Mode

In Shutter Priority (time value, or Tv) mode, you select the shutter speed manually and the camera will automatically select the correct aperture value for a correct exposure. Set this mode by pressing the mode button and turning the Main Dial until [Tv] is displayed on the camera's LCD panel. The EOS-3 offers you the exceptionally wide range of choices in shutter speed, from 30 seconds all the way up to an astonishing 1/8000 second. Shutter speeds are selected by using the Main Dial to scroll through the values until the desired speed is displayed on the camera's LCD panel. In its default settings, the camera allows you to select shutter speeds in 1/3-stop increments. If you prefer to make your adjustments in 1/2-stop increments, you can use Custom Function 6 to change this setting to Position 2.

The shutter speed selected is displayed in both the LCD panel and the viewfinder. The appropriate aperture setting, selected by the camera based on the light value determined by the metering system, is also displayed in both locations. Even though aperture values are indicated in 1/3-stop increments, the aperture mechanism is actually adjusted in 1/8-stop increments for exceptionally accurate automatic exposure. If the aperture value flashes, this means that either the smallest or largest aperture of the lens in use

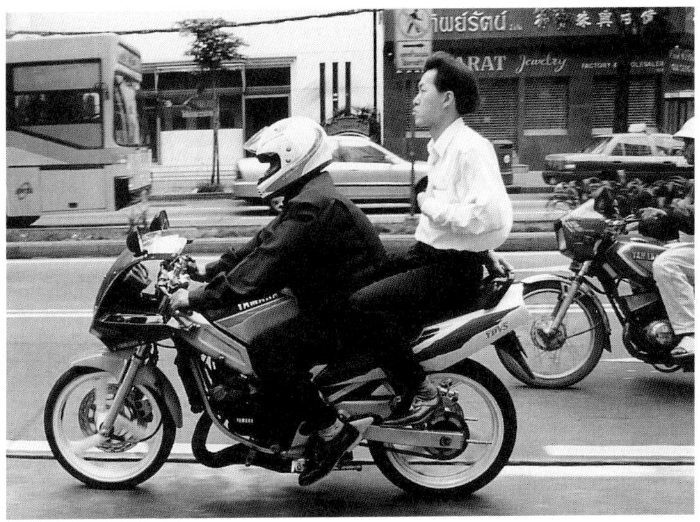

For this photograph, the photographer used Shutter Priority mode to select a sufficiently fast shutter speed to freeze the action.

is not sufficient for correct exposure. If you take the photograph anyway, it will be over- or underexposed. To correct this, you must choose a different shutter speed by turning the Main Dial until the aperture value no longer flashes. If you wish, you can use Custom Function 16 to switch automatically to a shorter or longer shutter speed to prevent improper exposure in such situations. When this safety shift is activated, the camera will automatically shift to a shorter shutter speed when the smallest aperture is insufficient to prevent overexposure and shift to a longer shutter speed when the largest aperture is insufficient to prevent underexposure. It is up to you, however, to pay attention and put the camera on a tripod or other support if this shift is to a shutter speed too slow for you to hand hold the camera. Remember that Canon's IS (image stabilized) lenses will allow you to handhold the camera a much slower shutter speeds than are possible with ordinary lenses.

Shutter Priority mode is ideal for action photography, because it allows you to pick a fast shutter speed to freeze action. It also allows you to pick a slow shutter speed when you want a blurred image to suggest speed or for other artistic effect. Choosing a fast shutter speed also will provide a larger aperture for those times when limited depth of field is desired. Use this mode for taking photos of a television screen or a computer monitor, and choose a shutter speed of 1/15 second—but you'll need a tripod or other support for this to work.

Depending on the subject, Shutter Priority mode can be combined with other functions—for example, spot metering, AF mode, motor drive speed, exposure compensation, automatic bracketing, and so on. For most applications, we recommend AI Servo autofocus, evaluative metering, automatic choice of AF sensor, and Continuous Motor Drive mode.

Shutter Speed and Subject Motion

If the shutter speed is not fast enough when photographing action, the resulting photo will be more or less blurred. Should you want sharp images with no visible blur, then setting the correct shutter speed is vital. Which speed to use depends on the speed of subject motion and the direction of motion with respect to the camera. An example is a person running at a distance of about 16 feet (5 m) from the camera: If the person is running obliquely (at a slant) to the camera axis, then a 1/500 or faster shutter speed should be set; if the person is running parallel to the camera axis, it is generally safe to set a speed no slower than 1/250 second; and if the person is running toward or away from the camera, you can generally get sharp results with a shutter speed of 1/125 or faster. These are general guidelines only, and it is always best to do tests before taking important photos. As a general rule, just remember that the faster the subject movement, the faster the shutter speed should be.

Aperture Priority (Av) Automatic Exposure Mode

Basically, Aperture Priority (Av, or aperture value) mode operates just the reverse of Shutter Priority (Tv) mode. As with the other modes, to activate Tv mode, press the mode button and turn the Main Dial until [Av] is displayed in the camera's LCD panel. Then select the desired aperture setting, and the camera selects the

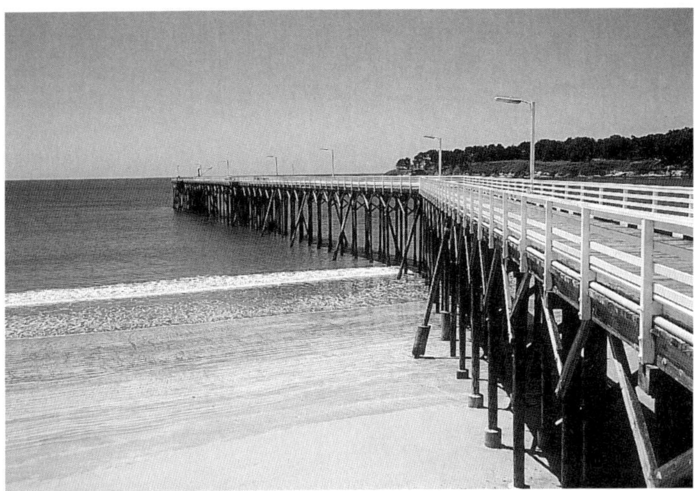

Aperture Priority mode was used here to allow the photographer complete control over depth of field.

appropriate shutter speed based on the light level. This gives you control over the amount of depth of field in your photographs.

Use the Main Dial to choose the aperture setting. In the factory default settings, turning the dial lets you scroll through available aperture values in 1/3-stop increments; you can use Custom Function 6 to provide aperture values in 1/2 stops or in full stops only. As you choose aperture values, the camera automatically selects the appropriate shutter speed in the range between 1/8000 and 30 seconds. Even though the indicators in the viewfinder and LCD panel display only 1/3-stop values, the shutter speed is actually chosen in 1/8-stop increments for exceptionally accurate exposure.

Because the shutter speed range is much greater than the available aperture values, incorrect exposures are not likely in normal use. But the camera can select very long shutter speeds at times, so you must be alert to the possibility of blurring if too long a shutter speed is indicated. If, in spite of the great range of shutter speeds, the speed selected by the camera blinks, this indicates incorrect exposure and you must change the aperture setting until the shutter-speed indicators no longer blink. If 1/8000 is indicated and blinks, then you must choose a smaller aperture to prevent overexposure. If you do not wish to alter the aperture, you can add a neutral-density filter to the front of the lens to cut down on the amount of light without altering depth of field. As with Tv mode, you can use Custom Function 16 to activate a safety shift function for Av mode. The camera will then automatically set a smaller or larger aperture to avoid incorrect exposure.

For general photography with Av mode, we recommend evaluative metering, one shot autofocus, and automatic selection of the AF sensor.

Because it allows purposeful control of depth of field, Av mode is particularly useful for portrait, landscape, still life, and architectural photography. Evaluative metering handles most of these subjects without any difficulty, providing perfect exposures. With very strong backlighting or very high subject contrast, however, either exposure compensation or the use of evaluative metering may be required for precise exposure accuracy. This is particularly true with portrait subjects in front of very dark or very light backgrounds, where spot or multispot metering can be used to provide correct exposure.

Aperture Numbers (F/Stops)

The indicated aperture number (f/2, for example) is actually the denominator of a fraction, which should properly be expressed as 1/2. This fraction is the ratio (as a ratio, it is expressed as 1:2) of the apparent diameter of the lens aperture as viewed from the front to the focal length of the lens. As an example, a 50 mm lens with an aperture of f/2 would have an apparent aperture of 25 mm. Similarly, the same lens set to f/4 would then have an apparent aperture of 12.5 mm. The sizes are measured with special optical instruments. By convention, lens makers long ago dropped the first number in this ratio or fraction to save space and avoid confusion, so rather than seeing :2, 1:4, and so forth on your aperture indicator, you simply see 2, 4, and so forth. This is the reason that larger numbers indicate smaller apertures, something that can be confusing to the beginner.

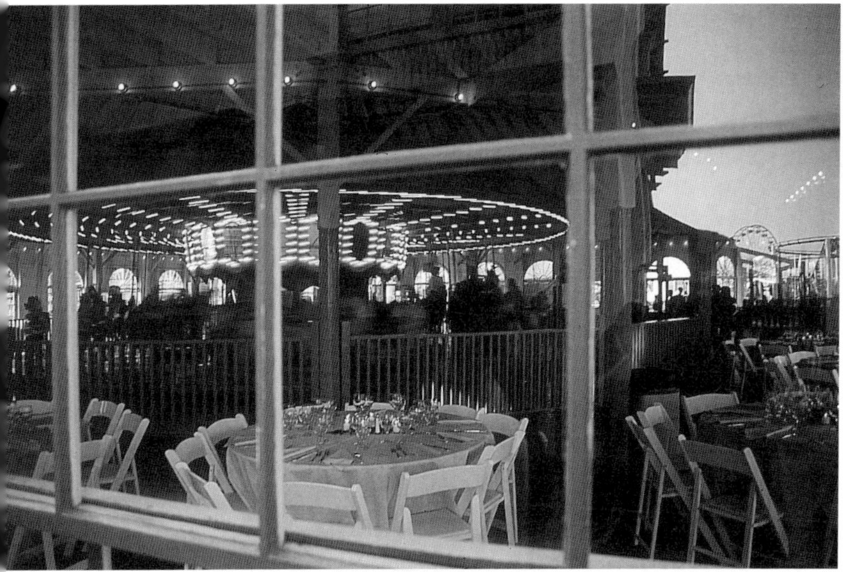

Manual mode was used in this photograph so the photographer had total control over the rendering of the various elements in the scene.

Manual Mode (M)

Any camera that will draw the attention of professional photographers must offer a fully manual exposure mode, whether they actually use it. Many professionals will tell amateurs that they never use exposure automation, but if you watch them at work you will often find their cameras set to Av, Tv, or even P. The fact is that the Canon EOS-3 is so good in determining exposure automatically that there really is rarely any reason to second guess the camera and revert to full manual control. In fact, today the fully manual mode may be of more importance to the amateur who wants to learn more of the technical aspects of photography by switching off the automation.

In Manual mode, both shutter speed and aperture are adjusted using the Main Dial and Quick Control Dial. Exposure may be determined by referring to the light meter indicator in the viewfinder or by use of a separate, handheld exposure meter.

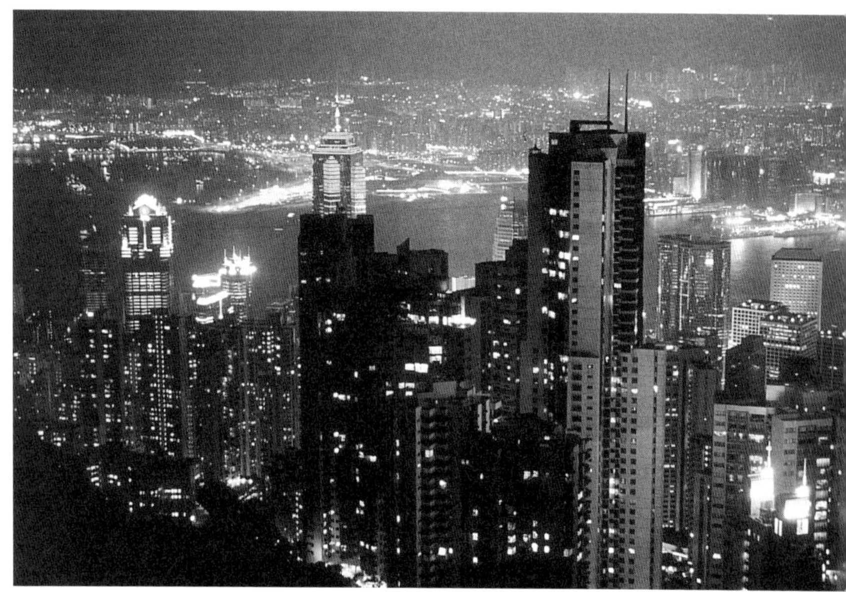

For exposure times longer than 30 seconds, set the camera to Bulb mode.

To switch the camera to Manual mode, press the mode button and turn the Main Dial until the symbol [M] appears on the LCD panel. Normally, you will then adjust the shutter speed with your index finger on the Main Dial and the aperture with your thumb on the Quick Control Dial (remembering, of course, to turn it on with the switch just above it). If you wish to reverse this—to control the aperture with your index finger and the shutter speed with your thumb—you can change this with Custom Function 5. In the factory default settings, both values can be adjusted in 1/3-stop increments. If you prefer half-stop or whole-stop increments, you can change this with Custom Function 6.

A photographer will generally work by choosing a shutter speed or an aperture value based on the sort of subject and the desired look of the photograph, and then adjust the other value to get proper exposure. Deviation from these exposure values is shown on the scale on the right inside the viewfinder. The scale has a central marker, which indicates correct exposure. By turning either control dial, or both, you can move an indicator to the right of the bar graph scale until it aligns with the central indicator. This sets the camera for correct exposure.

Manual mode lets you select metering and motor drive options to suit the situation. Often, it is combined with manual focus to deal with particularly difficult photographic situations, such as backlighted subjects that are difficult for the autofocus to work with. In addition, the indicated correct exposure may not always be the right exposure when you are after special effects, such as high-hey or low-key images, expanded tonal ranges, multiple exposures, experimental photos, or photos taken with very dark filters or special-effect filters. And, of course, you will usually want to work with manual focus when working with infrared film, because the plane of focus indicated by visible light does not correspond to the plane of focus for infrared.

Bulb (Time Exposure) Mode

With the Canon EOS-3, you have two possible ways of taking time exposures: automatically or manually. In Shutter Priority (Tv) mode, you can set shutter speeds as long as 30 seconds and rely on the camera to select the appropriate lens aperture. Using Manual mode, you have a similar range of adjustment and must determine the appropriate lens aperture either with the camera's meter or a separate hand exposure meter.

Exposures longer than 30 seconds are possible by using the camera's Bulb mode, accessed by pressing the mode button and turning the Main Dial until [buLb] is displayed on the LCD panel. In Bulb mode, the shutter will remain open as long as pressure is maintained on the shutter release button, although it makes much more sense to do this with the Remote Switch RS-80N3 or the Timer Remote Controller TC-80N3. These connect to the remote socket on the left end of the camera, making long time exposures of any duration possible. Understand, though, that even with a camera like the EOS-3, which draws very little current during this operation, frequent use of Bulb mode will shorten battery life.

You can use the camera to time your bulb exposures by watching the LCD panel, which will count up to 30 seconds in

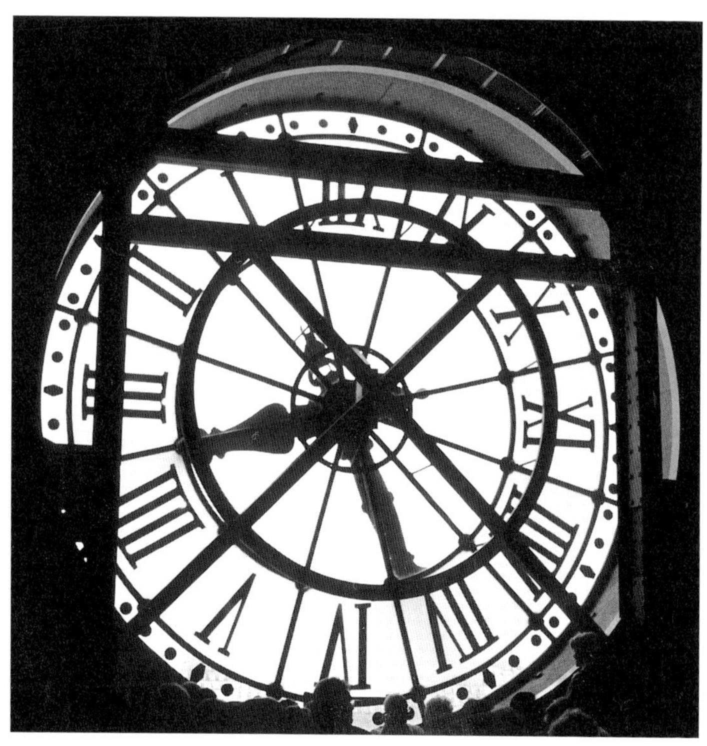

Manual metering mode was used to assure the silhouetted appearance of the clock in Musée d'Orsay, in Paris. Photograph by Rebecca Saltzman.

the area of the frame counter and will then denote each 30 second increment with a set of bars protruding from the film cassette icon. Times longer than the camera can display can be tracked with a stopwatch or wristwatch. Long exposures are often useful for fireworks at night or a starlit sky. Night photographs with multiple manual "pops" from an electronic flash can also produce interesting results. (See also page 64.)

Multiple Exposures

When you set the EOS-3 for multiple exposures, the film advance motor is switched off for the number of frames you set so all of these images are recorded on the same frame of film.

The camera can be set for up to nine multiple exposures, but by "tricking" the camera any number or images can be placed on one frame. The button for activating multiple exposures is under the flap at the right of the camera and marked with an icon of overlapping frames. When you press this button, the multiple exposure icon appears on the LCD panel along with the number 1. Use the Main Dial to set this to the desired number of multiple exposures between 1 and 9. As a reminder that multiple exposure mode is engaged, the multiple exposure icon remains on the LCD panel, and flashes after the first of the exposure series. The counter starts at the number you have set and counts down, always showing the number of exposures remaining. These numbers are also displayed in the viewfinder on the lower right. If you wish to cancel the multiple exposure mode once set, press the multiple exposure button again and dial the number on the LCD panel back to 1. Although the film advance motor is turned off when this mode is engaged, near the beginning and end of a roll the film may still move slightly, so images requiring critical registration of multiple exposures should be taken in the middle of the roll of film. If you wish to place more than nine exposures on one frame, set the multiple exposure mode to 9; when it has counted down and displays 1, press the multiple exposure button again and dial in the additional exposures you want. You can repeat this an infinite number of times to put any desired number of frames onto the film frame.

The hard part of multiple exposures is exposure metering.

When working with a black background, as at night, with little or no overlap of the subject recorded in each exposure, no compensation will be required and normal metering procedures for a subject against a black background apply. However, when subjects overlap, compensation must be made to prevent gross overexposure. The usual rule of thumb is to divide the overall exposure by the number of exposures to get perfect exposure where all exposures overlap elements. This is, however, only a starting point for exposure determination, and the photographer should always do his or her own tests prior to making any important images with multiple exposures.

An easy way to get approximately correct exposure is to multiply the number of exposures by the film speed and use the new speed when metering. As an example, three overlapping exposures on ISO 100 film would lead to an exposure index (EI) of 300. The closest available ISO setting on the camera is ISO 320, so this is what should be used. This cuts to 1/3 the amount of light reaching the film in each of the three exposures, for a composite total of 3/3, or full exposure. As we said, though, this is only a starting point for personal experimentation, but should be pretty close to the correct exposure. It is best to make multiple exposures on negative films, as they are more tolerant of exposure errors.

Electronic Flash

Photography with electronic flash is made very simple with the Canon EOS-3 camera, Canon's Evaluative Through the Lens (E-TTL) flash measurement system, and the EX series Canon flash units. Even the most difficult applications of electronic flash become child's play when this system is used correctly. There are still some photographers of the "old school" who refuse to use electronic flash because they believe pictures taken with it look unnatural. These photographers are missing a lot—particularly the advanced fill flash made possible by the E-TTL system, which measures both ambient light and flash and sets the proportion between the two for a natural look. Photos taken in darkness, fill

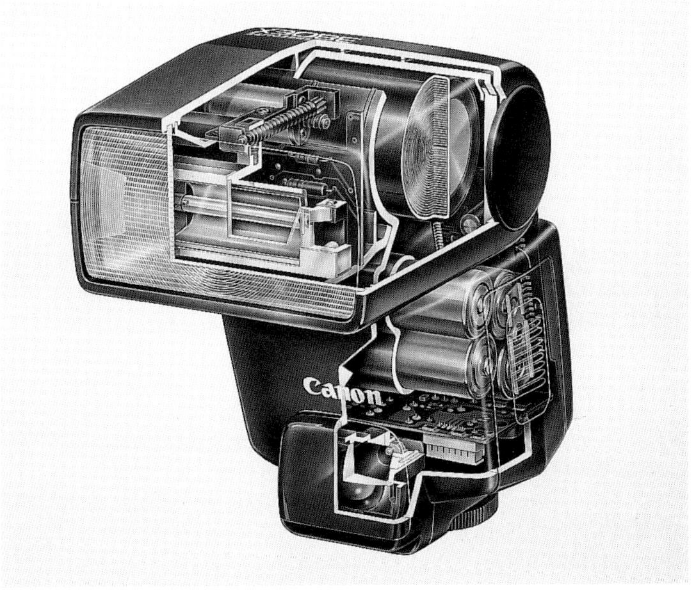

The Speedlite 380EX flash unit is particularly designed to work with the E-TTL evaluative metering system of the EOS-3, but is compatible with all Canon cameras.

flash photos, photos with backlighting—all can be taken with this system to produce excellent and natural-looking results. But to use this system properly, you must know which exposure and operational modes to use for which situations, such as altering the shutter speed or the aperture setting to change the picture's design and appearance.

About E-TTL

The E-TTL flash system on the Canon EOS-3, which is designed to balance light from the flash with existing light, is an extremely refined flash measuring system. It works with the same 21-area evaluative metering system described in the chapter on metering modes, but for flash, the weighting of the metering areas is different. For flash, the camera weighs the active AF sensor area as the main metering area, ignoring sensors in other areas; only the metering information from this area is used for the electronic flash measurement. For this reason, very bright or very dark backgrounds will not adversely affect the flash metering, because it will always be based on the main subject. Computation of the metering values is rapid, and results in photographs in which both the foreground and background are properly exposed.

Depending on the subject, the light from the flash is graduated in very fine increments and proportioned so that the look of natural light is not lost. Because ambient light is also analyzed by evaluative metering—and weighted on the AF sensor—a very natural look can be produced in which the flash serves simply to brighten up the shaded areas.

If the E-TTL system flash is used on the EOS-3 with the camera set in a different metering mode than evaluative metering, the ambient exposure is measured by the metering system using that mode, center-weighted average, partial, or spot metering. The flash is measured and adjusted by evaluative flash metering and weighted toward the active AF sensor. When using the older EZ series of flash units with the Canon EOS-3, the flash measurement is made using A-TTL (Advanced Through the Lens), which also includes ambient metering but without preflash for actual flash metering. A-TTL produces excellent results in most applications, but the fill flash will not be as finely tuned as with E-TTL. With other flash units, in most cases only simple TTL, without measurement of ambient light, is possible. In these situations, the light from the electronic flash is measured by a separate flash metering cell, which is divided into three areas. This cell measures flash only, not ambient light, and works with the EOS-3's computer to simply shut off the flash tube when a proper amount of light has reached the subject.

The E-TTL flash system is at its best with the new Canon Speedlite 550EX, which was specially designed for the EOS-3. E-TTL functions, however, with all EX series flash units, which currently include the 380EX and 220EX, in addition to the 550EX. Along with the 550EX, the photographer has available cordless remote E-TTL with multiple 550EX flash units mounted off-camera, a totally new system.

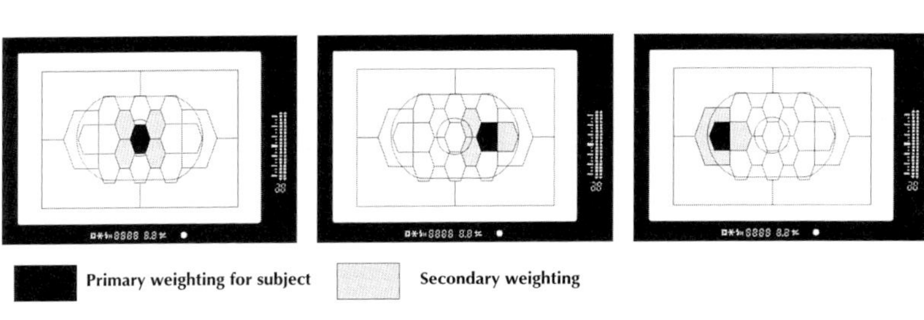

These diagrams illustrate the EOS-3's 21 evaluative metering zones for E-TTL flash. Flash metering is weighted on the active focusing point's metering zone.

Electronic Flash Functions

The EX series of flash units for the EOS-3 offer a wide variety of flash functions activated by buttons on the back panel of the flash units; some functions can also be controlled by settings on the camera.

The E-TTL automatic flash function is the default mode on the EOS-3 and the flash, and can be used effectively in all exposure modes except DEP. E-TTL uses autofocus-coupled evaluative metering with balanced fill flash, which produces the ideal mix of flash and ambient exposure in most situations.

High-speed-flash sync (FP) allows the use of fill flash in situations that would previously have been impossible. Because this mode can be used at shutter speeds between 1/250 and 1/8000 second, it is possible to use it outdoors with a wide aperture, such as f/1.4, to produce a blurred background behind the main subject.

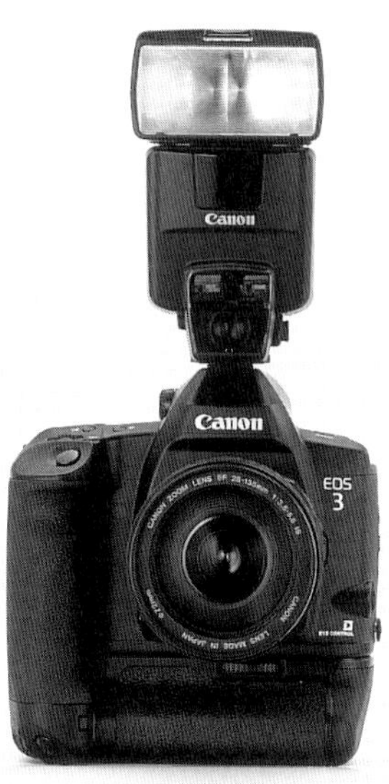

The Canon EOS-3 with the Canon Speedlite 550EX flash unit.

With slow-speed synchronization, which works all the way down to 30 seconds and Bulb setting, it is possible to expose the main subject and background correctly even in very dim light. This would be useful in posing someone in front of a window overlooking a city scene and getting a long enough exposure so that the city shows up instead of just a dead black space where the window is.

With electronic flash exposure lock (FEL), it is possible to lock the output of the flash to a preselected value. In this case, the flash exposure corresponds to the value obtained at the active AF sensor area. (Use Custom Function 13 to limit the number of focusing points selectable manually or by eye to 11.)

Electronic flash exposure compensation can be input manually within the range of +/–3 EV. Thus, you can intentionally reduce or increase the output of the flash in 1/3-stop increments to produce certain effects.

Electronic flash auto bracketing is available at this time only with the Speedlite 550EX and the FEB (Flash Exposure Bracketing) setting, which does the same thing with electronic flash that AEB mode does with ambient light.

Cordless E-TTL flash control combines the precision of E-TTL exposure determination with the convenience of off-camera and multiple-flash photography.

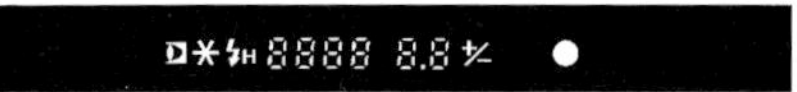

Viewfinder information showing flash-ready indicator (lightning bolt) and use of high-speed sync (H).

Flash Information Displays

The flash information displays, which are on the back of the flash units, give such information as flash function mode and flash distance range. Inside the viewfinder of the EOS-3 is a flash bolt symbol, which lights to indicate that the flash unit has fully recycled and is ready to fire. When high-speed-flash sync is being used, an [H] appears next to this indicator to advise that this special mode is in use.

Guide Number

The guide number is a rating of the power of the flash when used with a given film speed. The higher the guide number, the more powerful the flash. Guide numbers serve well as a simple, one-number means of comparison of the maximum power output of flash units.

Though flash automation makes it rarely necessary, if you do want to calculate the exposure manually, divide the distance from flash to subject into the guide number. This will give you the lens aperture to use for best results. Be sure to use the same unit of measure (feet or meters) that the guide number is given in.

Electronic Flash Synchronization

The Canon EOS-3 is equipped with a vertical-travel, electromagnetically timed, bladed focal plane shutter. Such a shutter produces its highest shutter speeds by exposing just a narrow slit of film as the shutter moves across the film. If you try to take a photo with a standard electronic flash at these higher speeds, the flash will expose just a narrow strip of the film and not the whole image area. As shutter speeds are made slower, you will reach one in which the shutter opens fully and exposes the entire film frame before closing. That is the fastest speed at which that shutter can synchronize with standard electronic flash. With the EOS-3, this shutter speed is 1/200 second; at this speed, the camera will work fine with all sorts of electronic flash units, including large studio flash systems. All slower speeds are synchronized as well, so you may use them if you wish, remembering that if they are set too slow the ambient light will also affect the photo. With dedicated electronic flash units, the EOS-3 automatically sets the shutter speed, based on a combination of ambient and flash light.

It is also possible with the EX system flash units from Canon to use the flash at faster speeds, from 1/250 second all the way up to 1/8000 second, in Focal Plane mode (refers to the shutter type). In this mode, the electronic flash switches from producing a single pulse of light to producing a series of very rapid stroboscopic flashes (but the stroboscopic effect is so fast that it appears as a single flash to the eye), which expose the whole film frame sequentially as the shutter slit travels across the film. This produces the effect of high-speed synchronization, but reduces flash power.

Flash Exposure Lock (FEL)

With the flash exposure lock (FEL) button, located just to the left of the shutter release button, it is possible to store and hold a flash setting. The measuring area corresponds to the central spot metering circle. With Custom Function 13, it is possible to link the measuring area to the active AF sensors. This allows you to measure flash exposure on certain subject areas by putting the active measuring area on the part of the subject you wish to set

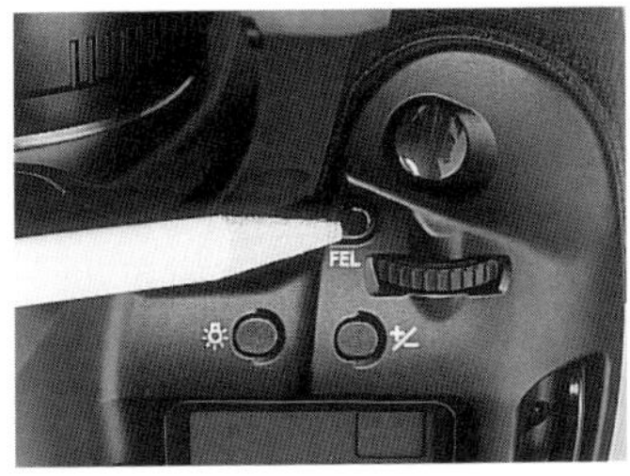

Use the FEL button to store and hold a flash setting.

the flash exposure from and pressing the FEL button. The flash fires at very reduced power (1/32nd power) to conserve the batteries; the measurement is made from the light reflected back from the subject area chosen. You will see [FEL] in the viewfinder for about half a second, as well as on the LCD panel. The information from this test flash is stored and used for subsequent exposures so long as partial pressure is maintained on the shutter release button and the viewfinder indicators remain visible. If you wish to cancel it before the camera automatically cancels it when the viewfinder and LCD panel information disappear, press the AF or mode button.

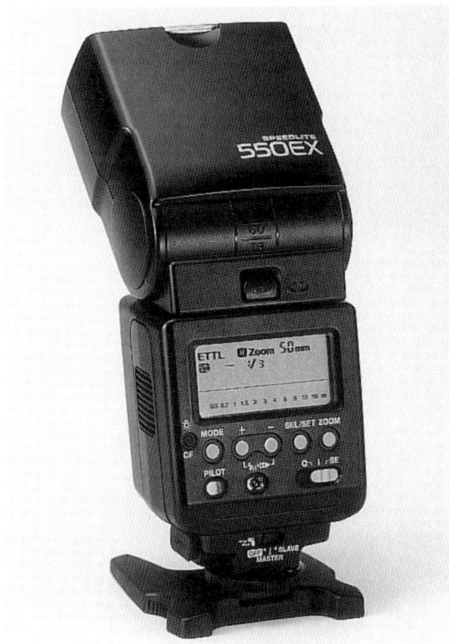

The Speedlite 550EX features auto zoom, FP flash, FEL, wireless flash photography, and more.

Indirect Flash

Direct frontal on-camera flash is very harsh, hard lighting. It is not pleasing, particularly when photographing people. For this reason, the flash head on many models of Canon Speedlite flash units can be tilted to point in other directions. This allows the use of bounce, or indirect, flash, in which the flash light is bounced from a ceiling, wall, or other reflective surface, producing a much softer light with less harsh shadows. In indirect flash, it is important that the ceiling, wall, or other surface from which the light is bounced be white or at least a neutral color. Otherwise, the flash light will take on the color of the reflective surface and impart that color to your subject. With the EX series of Speedlight flash units, full E-TTL and A-TTL flash operation is maintained when you're using indirect flash.

Flash Operation in Program Mode

Program mode is the simplest mode of camera operation for use with flash. With the 550EX flash mounted on the camera and switched on, you can be ready to take virtually any photo very quickly; just make sure that the flash-ready indicator in the viewfinder is lighted and that the flash is set for E-TTL operation. (See page 120 for a discussion of the 550EX.)

In Program mode, the Canon EOS-3 will automatically set the shutter speed based on the ambient lighting but will not exceed the 1/200 limit on standard E-TTL flash synchronization. In this mode, Program shift does not function. Manual flash exposure compensation can be set on the camera or on the flash. Also, flash exposure lock with the FEL button is possible.

Focal length and angle of view: The top photo was taken with an 80mm lens with a 30° angle of view. The bottom photo was taken with a 135mm lens, which yielded an angle of view of 18°.

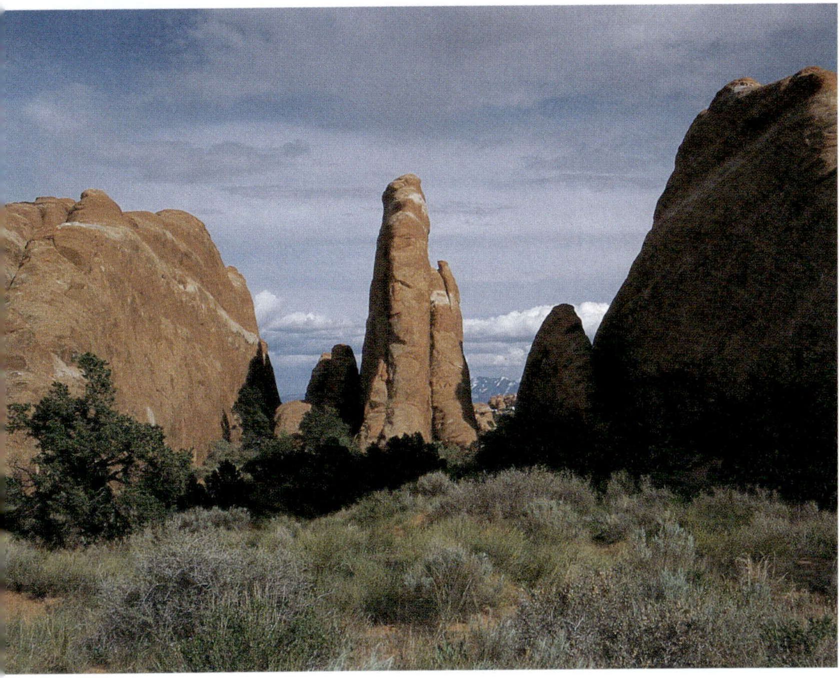

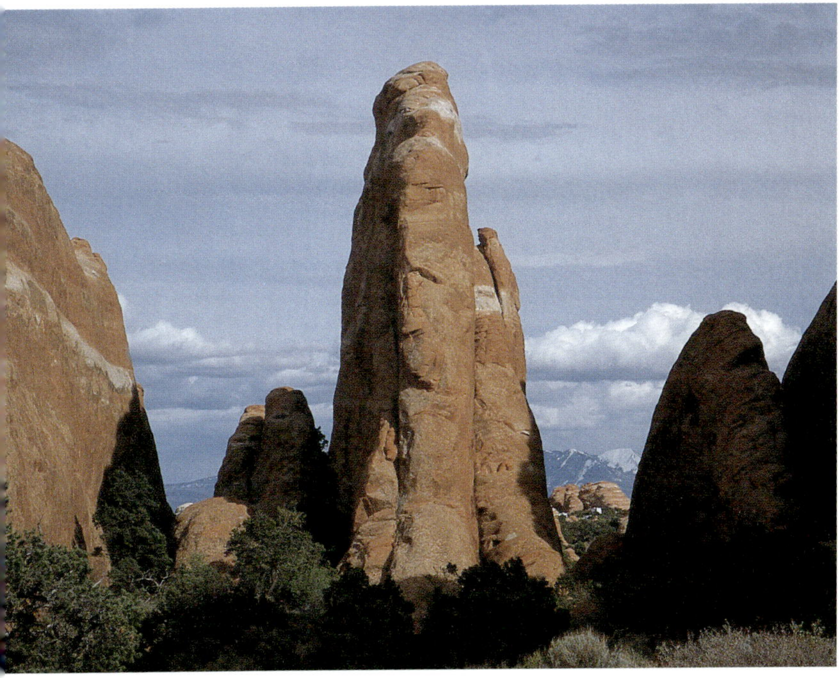

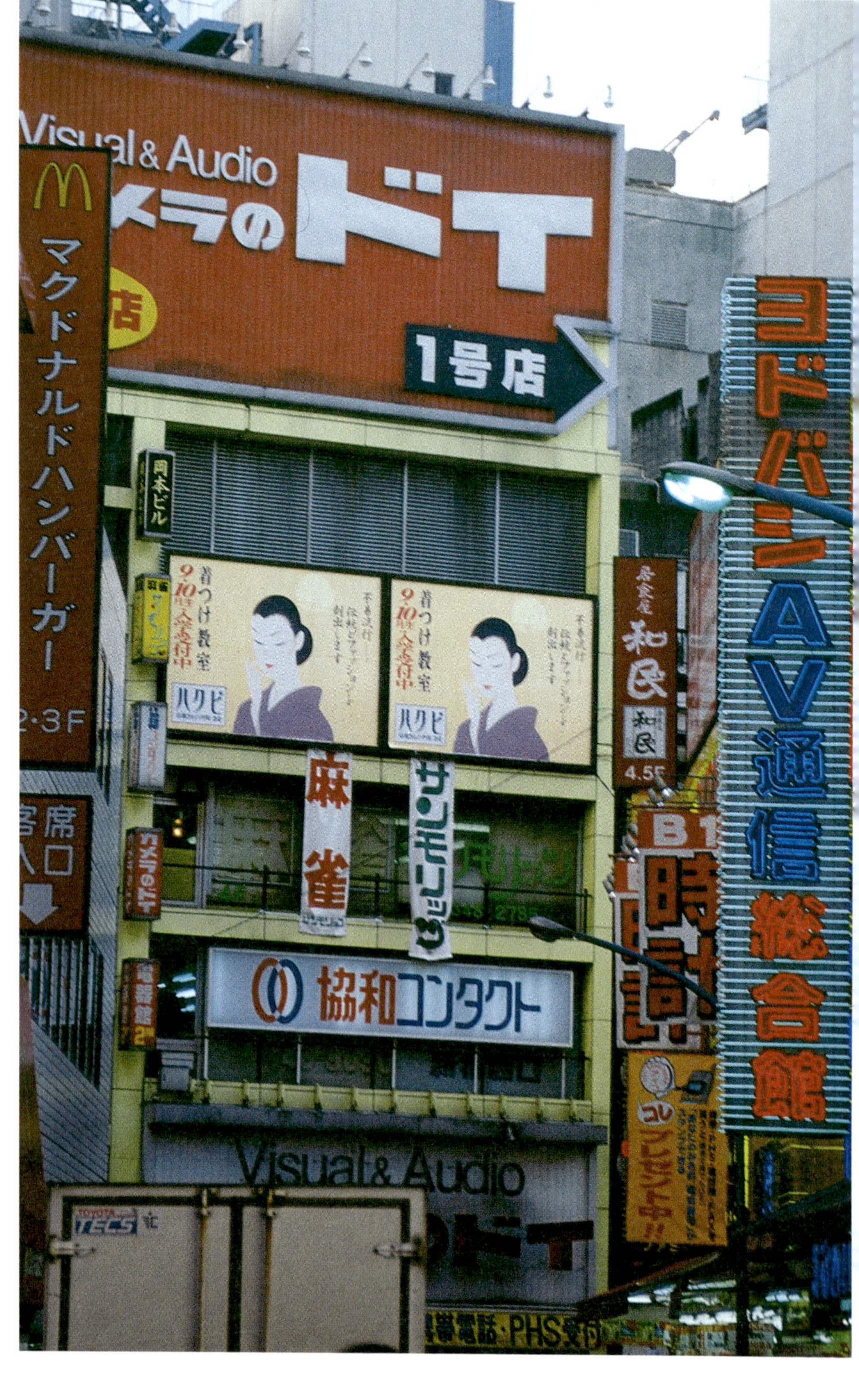

Visual & Audio
メラのドイ
1号店
マクドナルドハンバーガー
2·3F
客席入口
岡本ビル
着つけ教室
9·10月入会受付中
ハクビ
麻雀
サンモリッツ
和民
4.5F
B1
時計
ヨドバシAV通信総合館
協和コンタクト
プレゼント中!!
Visual & Audio
電話・PHS受付

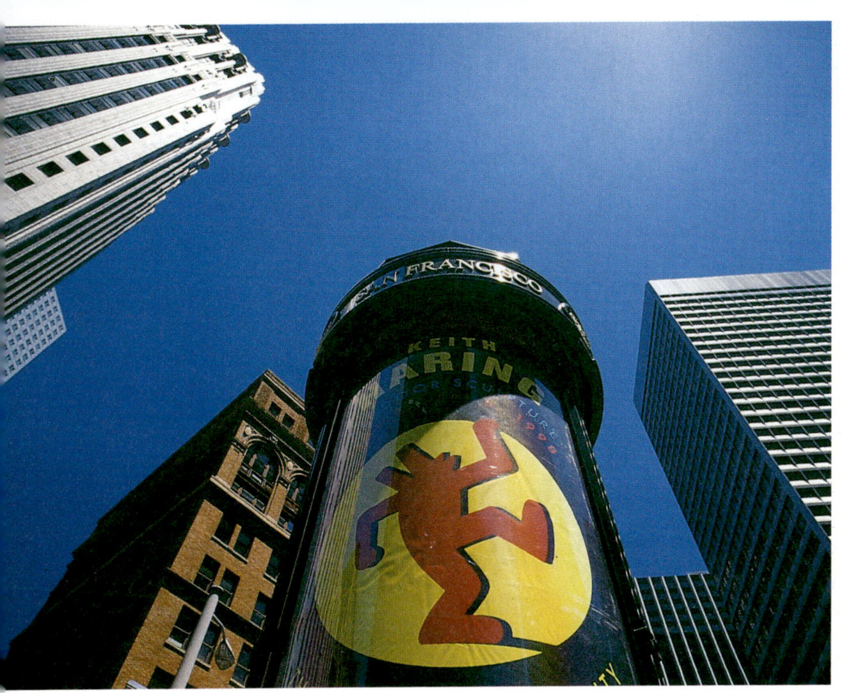

Above: This photo, taken with a 20mm lens, illustrates the exaggeration of perspective exhibited by the use of a wide-angle lens.

Left: An interesting study of color and typography shot with a 200mm lens. Notice the flatness and foreshortening of the subject, which are inherent in pictures taken with a telephoto.

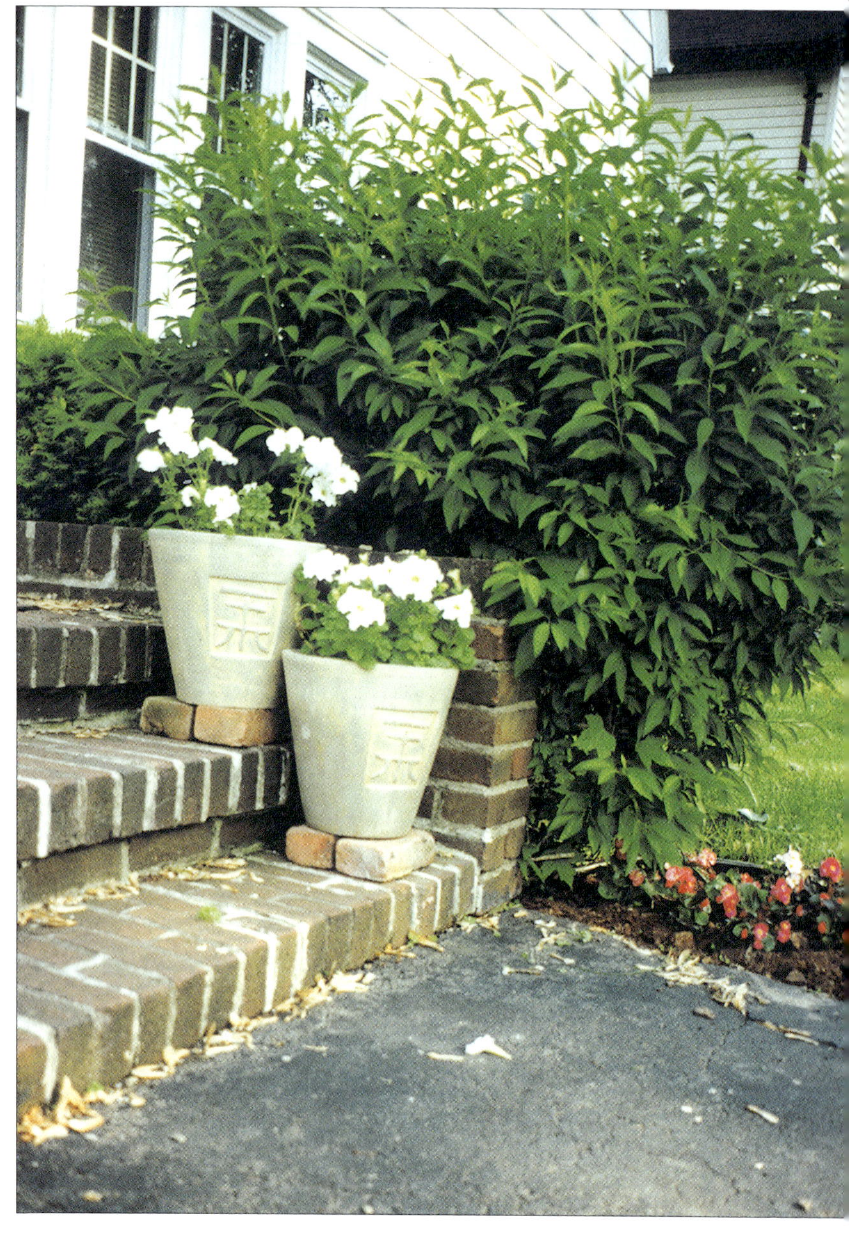

Program mode was used for this snapshot of a spring planting. Photo by A. T. Keys.

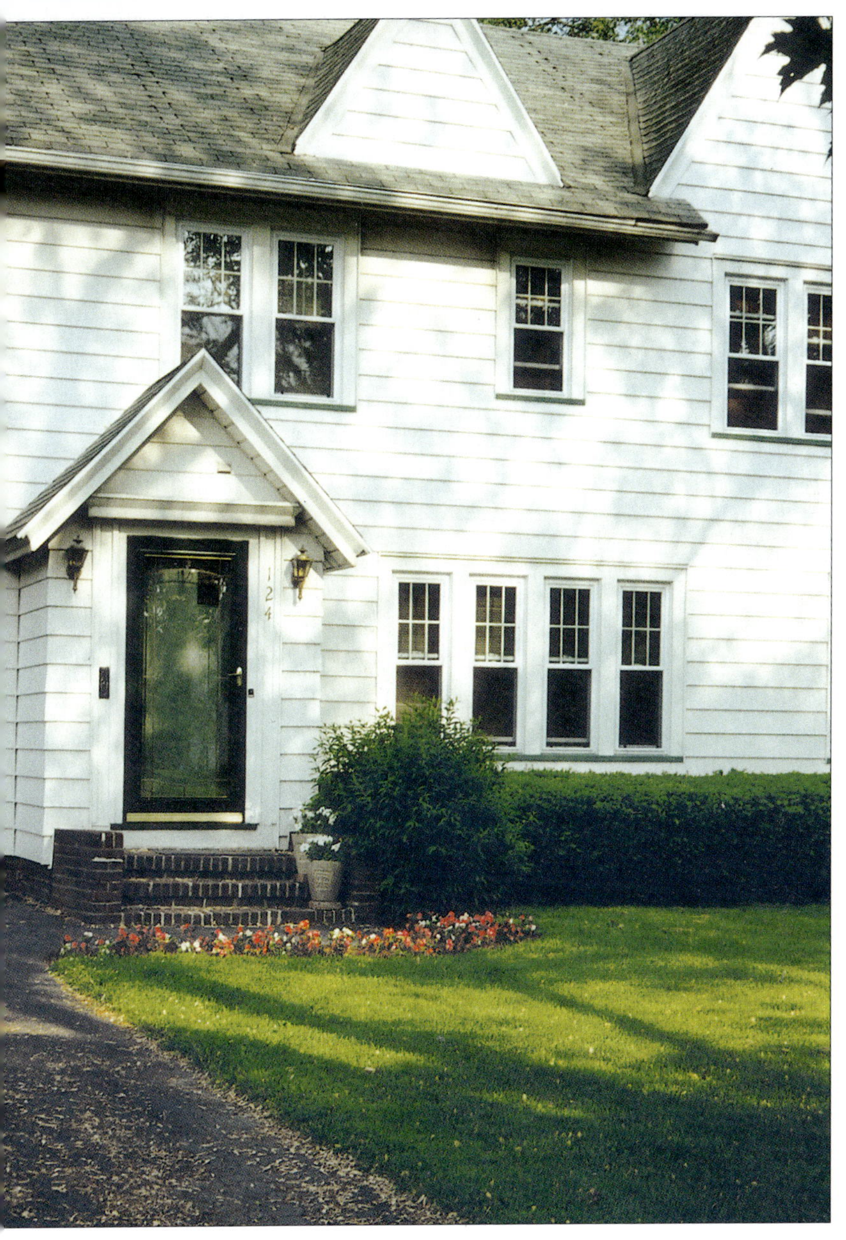

When photographing buildings, keep the film plane parallel with the building to prevent parallax problems. Photo by A. T. Keys.

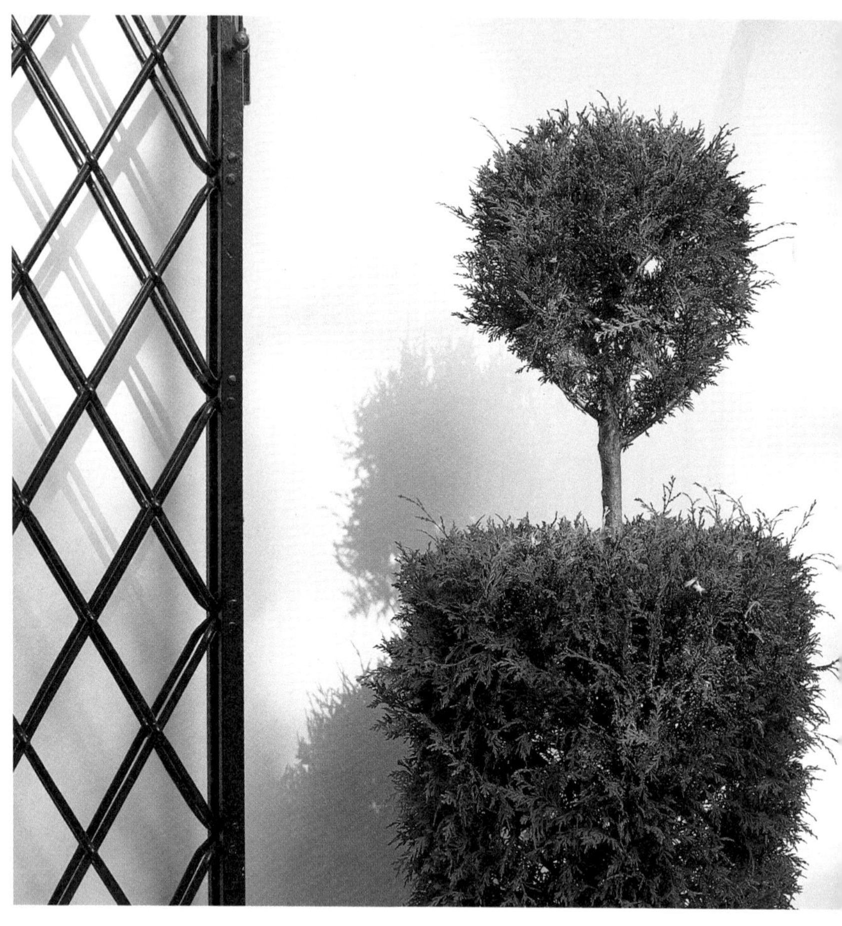

Above: A study in arrangement, pattern, and shadow easily captured by the advanced technology of the Canon EOS-3.

Right: Manual focus was used for this photo taken through broken glass, so the photographer could control the rendering of all of the elements in the composition.

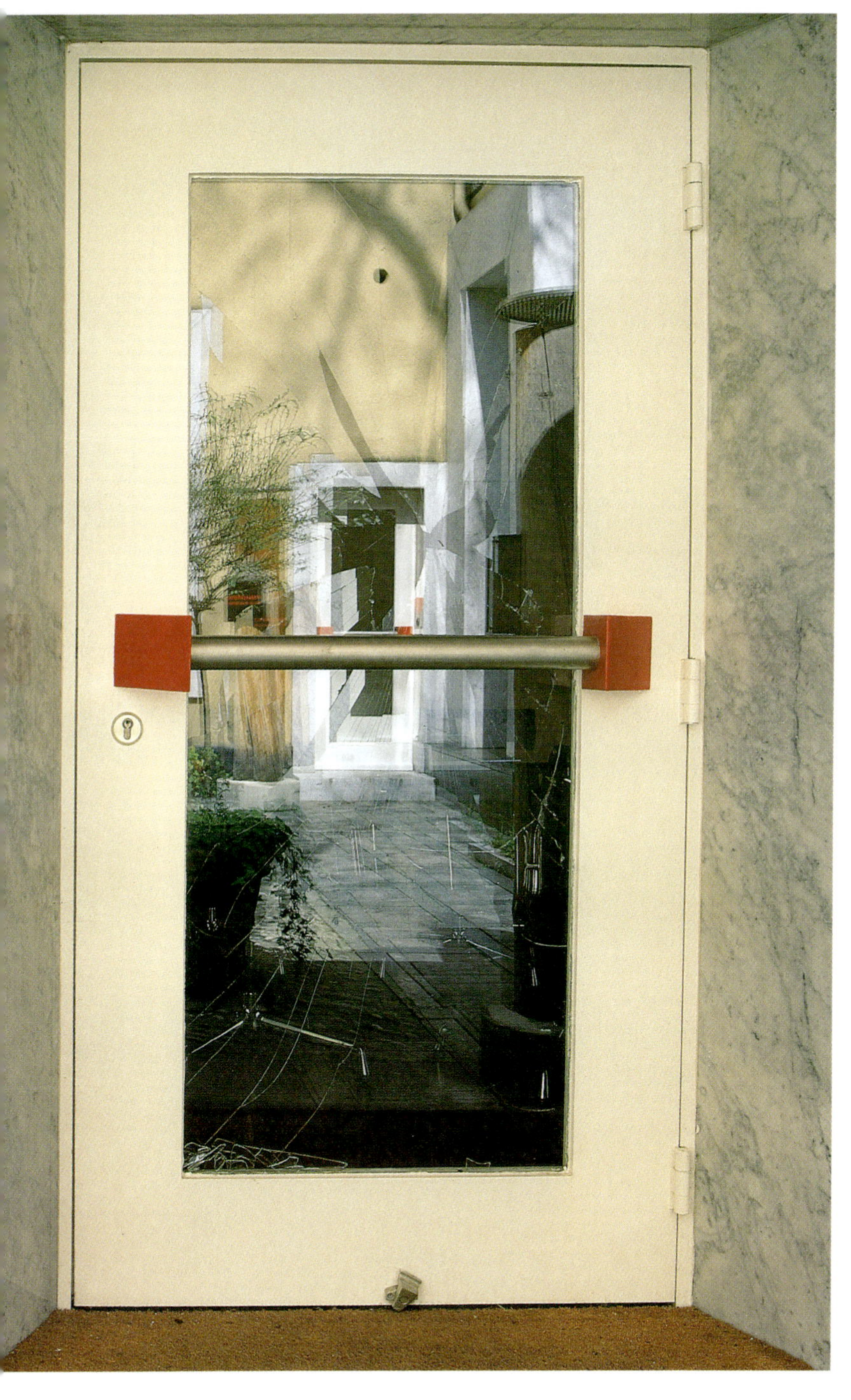

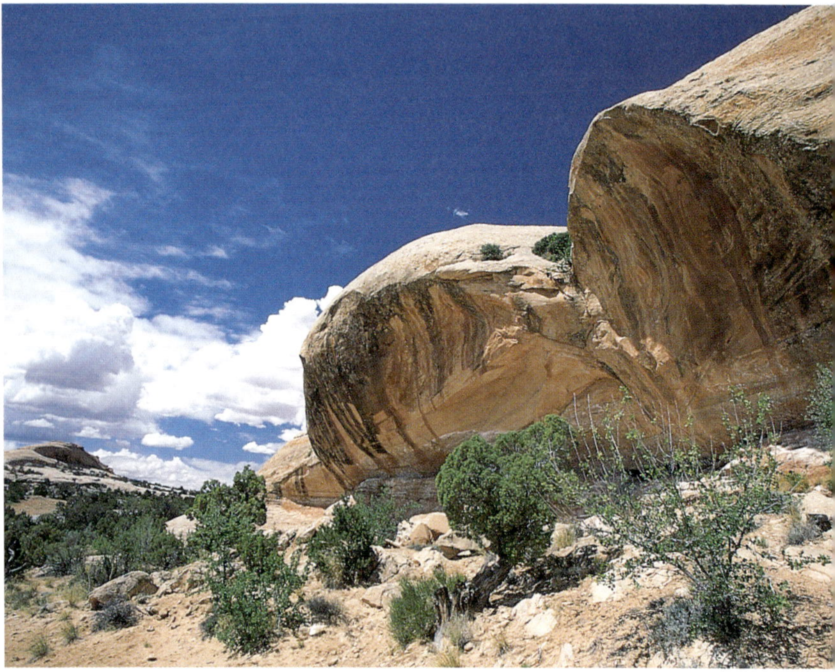

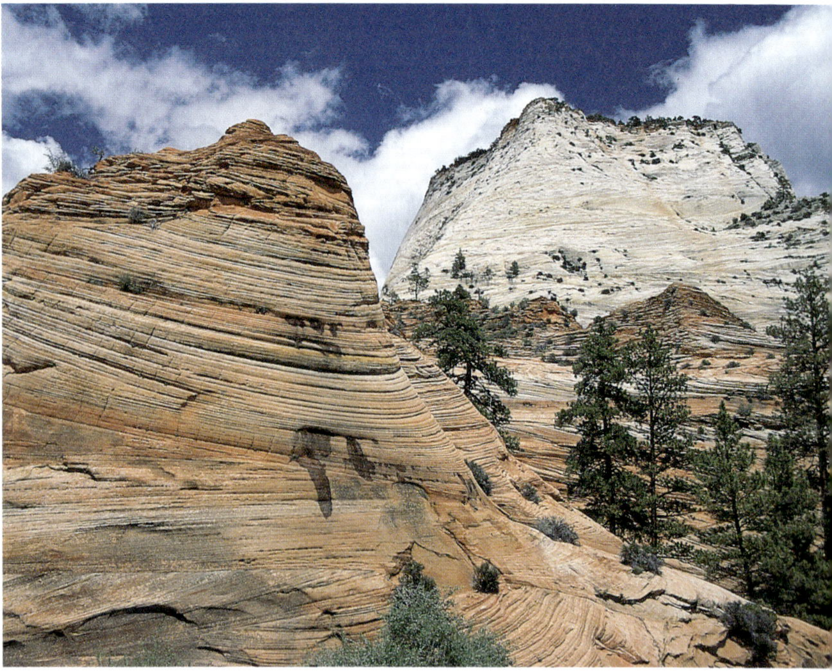

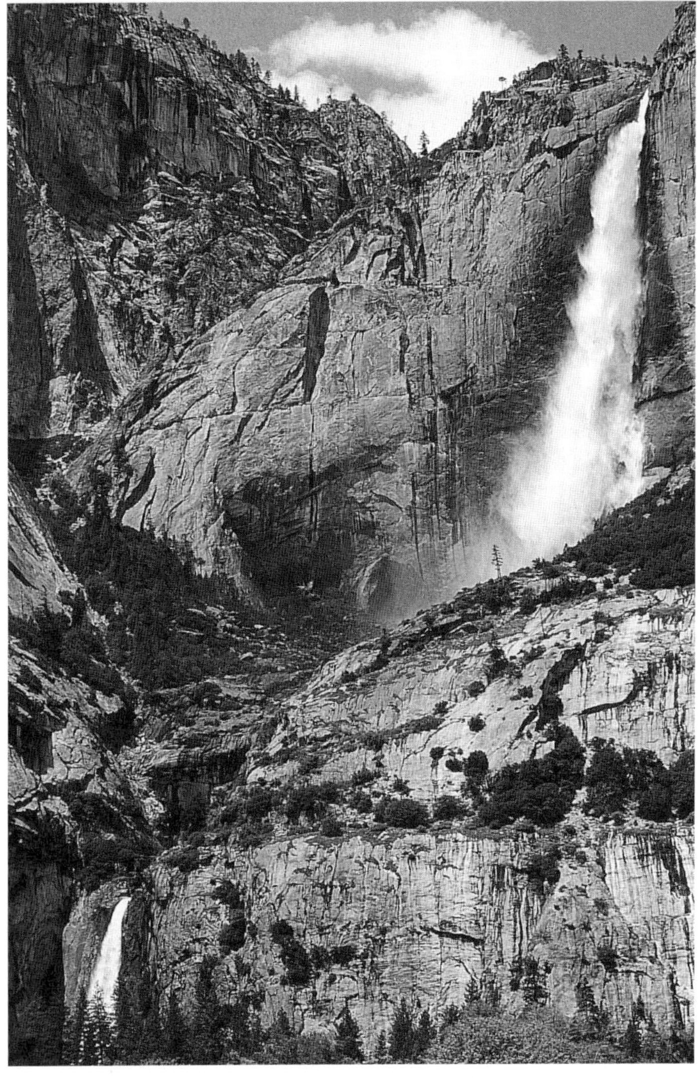

Above: The photographer used Shutter Priority mode to optimize the rendering of the waterfalls in this dramatic mountain scene.

At left: A circular polarizer was used in these landscape photographs to capture the tans of the rock formations against the intensely blue sky.

With flash, the background exposure can be controlled using the shutter speed. A short exposure time will not record much ambient light exposure, producing a dark background.

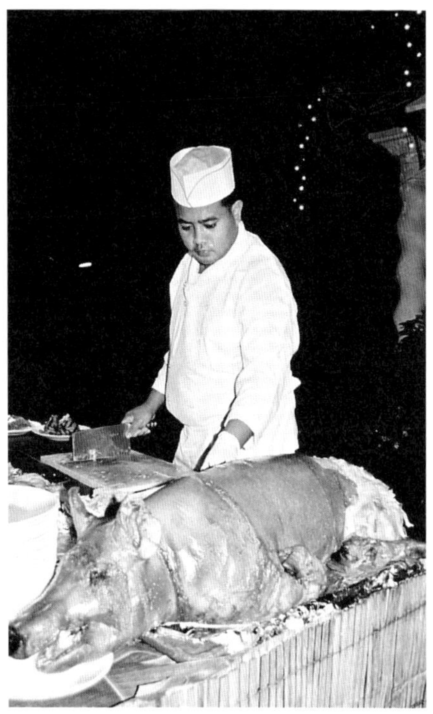

Flash Operation in Shutter Priority (Tv) Mode

The use of E-TTL with high-speed-flash sync in Tv mode offers a variety of interesting possibilities. First, though, because Program shift does not function when using a Canon Speedlite with the camera's Program mode, it is not possible to use the Program mode to obtain a specific shutter speed. If the situation requires a specific shutter speed, it is best to switch to Shutter Priority (Tv) mode. In this mode, you select the shutter speed, and the camera's metering system automatically selects and sets the complementary aperture setting. You can select the shutter speed you want either before or after switching the flash on. If you have set a shutter speed faster than 1/200 second prior to turning the flash on, however, the system will switch it back to 1/200 second when the flash is turned on. If you set the shutter speed after turning the flash on, you will find that it is impossible to select a speed faster than 1/200 second. With Custom Function 6, you can select the increments in which one click of the Main Dial changes the speed, either 1/3 stop (the factory default setting), 1/2 stop, or one full stop.

If you wish to use high-speed-flash sync with shutter speeds faster than 1/200 second, you must change the setting on the flash to High-Speed Sync mode. You do this by pressing the + and – buttons on the back of the flash simultaneously. You will then see an icon with a flash bolt and an H next to the E-TTL indication on the upper left of the LCD panel on the flash; an H is also displayed next to the flash bolt flash-ready indicator in the viewfinder. You are now free to set any shutter speed faster than 1/200 second all the way to the camera's maximum speed of 1/8000 second. You will also notice that the distance range of the flash, as displayed on its LCD panel, becomes shorter as you move to faster shutter speeds, so at the fastest speeds you will need to be close to your subject or use a high-speed film.

The camera will select an appropriate aperture for the best exposure based on the ambient light. Manual flash exposure compensation and FEL both work in this mode. High Speed Flash mode may be switched off by pressing the + and – buttons on the back of the flash twice simultaneously.

Most important in the Tv exposure mode is that by manual selection of the shutter speed you have the possibility to intentionally alter the exposure of the background. As an example, consider a portrait of a person in front of a window. By selection of the shutter speed you can vary the view out the window from very light to very dark, while the E-TTL flash will always correctly expose your main subject. You must remember, however, that when using slow shutter speeds, blurring can happen—so you must instruct your subject to remain as still as possible. Just make sure that the main subject remains in the range of the flash.

Blurring the Background

Like us, we're sure you've seen many images over the years in which a sharply delineated subject stands against a blurred background. This effect can be obtained by setting the Canon EOS-3 to a slow shutter speed (generally 1/15 second or slower) and panning the camera with a moving subject. The ambient exposure is set to expose the background depending on the desired effect. This kind of photograph requires practice and experience on the part of the photographer in determining the appropriate shutter speed based on background illumination and the desired look of the final photograph.

Flash Operation in Aperture Priority (Av) Mode

The ease of operation and automation of the E-TTL flash operation can also be used in Aperture Priority mode, also called Av (aperture value) mode. In this mode, you select the lens aperture setting you wish to use and the camera selects the appropriate shutter speed based on ambient light. This gives you control over the depth of field in your photographs with fill flash. As always in the Av mode, you set the aperture you want by using the Main Dial. By means of Custom Function 6, you can change the exposure increments for one dial click from 1/3 stop (the factory default setting) to 1/2 stop or full stops. The camera will then select the appropriate shutter speed based on the light level between 1/200 second and 30 seconds. You can also use the high-speed-flash sync to allow the camera to select speeds faster than 1/200 second if the light level allows. You might need this, for example, when shooting a portrait against a very bright background, or if you wish to have the aperture nearly wide open to restrict depth of field and throw a distracting background out of focus. In Av mode, you can use FEL as well as high-speed-flash sync. High-speed-flash sync can also be used for photos of frozen motion.

Flash Operation in Manual Mode

The E-TTL flash control system also works during Manual mode, precisely delivering flash to the main subject, as is done in the other exposure modes. Note that using electronic flash combined with manual exposure is best done by experienced photographers. They will understand how to control all aspects of the image by choice of aperture setting, shutter speed setting, and the addition of carefully planned flash. During manual exposure

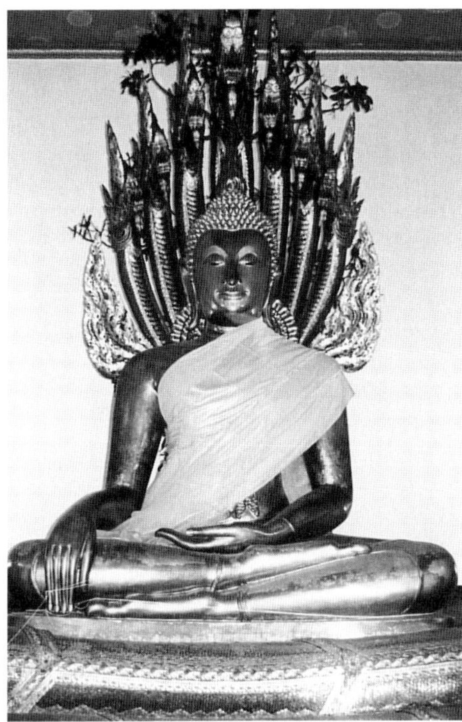

If exposure compensation had not been set, the white cloth would have fooled the meter and caused the photo to be underexposed.

setting with E-TTL flash control, shutter speeds from 1/200 second to 30 seconds are available. The range of available aperture settings depends, of course, on the lens in use. If shutter speeds faster than 1/200 second are selected before the flash is turned on, the camera switches to 1/200 second when the flash is switched on. If faster speeds are required, the flash must first be set for high-speed-flash sync. Both aperture and shutter speeds can be switched with Custom Function 6 to yield 1/3-stop settings (the factory default), 1/2-stop settings, or full-stop settings. It is also possible to switch the flash from E-TTL and use it manually by setting the desired power.

An example of the sort of photo that might require manual settings is an architectural scene in which the interior of a room as well as the area outside the windows and through an open door must all be exposed properly. Almost any good TTL flash system will expose the interior of the room correctly, but will usually cause the outdoor areas to be rendered very dark. If you adjust the flash to expose for the outdoors, the interior will be too light. In such a situation, it may be best to take an exposure meter reading outdoors and set the camera to expose that correctly, using a small lens aperture to provide plenty of depth of field, and then taking a flash meter reading with a handheld electronic flash meter and setting the flash unit(s) for proper exposure of the interior. This is the kind of image that a working professional photographer would spend a lot of time on, most certainly taking a series of bracketed exposures.

Other exposure possibilities for manual exposure with flash would include stopped motion in front of blur, and zoom effects in which a zoom lens is slowly zoomed during a long exposure while the flash has rendered the main subject sharp and frozen in time. You can even set the shutter on Bulb and take very long exposures with electronic flash picking out and freezing details.

Electronic Flash in Depth of Field Mode

Though the camera will fire the flash in DEP mode, it does not make any sense to do this because it defeats the action of this mode and reverts the camera to Program mode operation. In Program mode, the photo will be well exposed with proper flash balance but the depth of field will not correspond to the two DEP settings you have made.

Flash Exposure Compensation

Flash exposure compensation—unlike exposure compensation, which applies only to the ambient light and not to the flash—can be set either on the flash or on the camera. It affects only the amount of light delivered by the flash, with no effect on the camera's exposure setting for ambient light.

Flash exposure compensation is entered as follows. Press the +/– metering mode button on the top left of the camera and use the Quick Control Dial to dial in the desired compensation, in 1/3-stop increments, on the camera's LCD panel. After you have done this, only the +/– symbol appears on the LCD panel and in the viewfinder. If you switch the flash off or remove it from the camera, the +/– indicator in the viewfinder disappears, but the one on the main LCD panel stays as a reminder. You can also set the exposure compensation on the 550EX flash itself by pressing the SEL/SET button on the back of the flash until the +/– symbol appears and flashes on the LCD panel on the flash, and using the + and – buttons to set the desired amount of compensation.

Cordless E-TTL Exposure Control

Cordless E-TTL makes it possible to control exposure with the E-TTL system and an unlimited number of 550EX flash units set up in up to three zones. For example, you can do a portrait with one set of lights on the subject, a second set on the background, and a third set from above acting as a hair light. A switch on the back of the flash foot on the 550EX flash allows you to set each flash as a master or as a slave unit. The flash chosen as the master will be the one mounted on the camera, and the others will be set as slaves so that they will fire when triggered by the master. Instead of using one of the flash units on the camera, they can all be mounted off camera and controlled by a Speedlite Transmitter ST-E2 on the camera. While the zones are limited to three for technical reasons, the number of 550EX flash units that can be in any of these zones is unlimited. All flash units can be set for +/– exposure to create desired lighting ratios; all flash functions, even high-speed-flash sync, are available in this totally cordless "studio."

Red-Eye

All of us have seen those family photos in which someone looking at the camera has bright glowing red eyes. This unattractive effect is caused when light from the electronic flash on a camera goes into a person's eyes and bounces back from the retina. Because of its rich blood supply, the human retina is red, so this is the color the eyes take on. (The eyes of cats, due to their different structure, will look blue or green when this happens.) The red-eye effect results when the light from the flash goes out in a beam too close to the lens axis and thus goes straight into the subject's eyes. Usually, Canon Speedlite flash units are tall enough to eliminate this effect, but it can be cut down or eliminated by using bounce flash or add-on flash diffusers. Red-eye is most common when people have dilated eyes in dim light, so making the room light as bright as possible also helps. You can also get the flash up higher by using a connecting hot-shoe cable and either holding the flash up by hand or mounting it on a stand or flash bracket such as those from Stroboframe®.

The Speedlite 550EX

The hot-shoe-mounted Speedlite 550EX—the ultimate system flash—works very well with the E-TTL flash automation of the EOS-3 and harmonizes with all of the camera's electronic flash functions. It is the optimal flash for the EOS-3 and extends the capabilities of the camera substantially.

The advanced exposure control afforded by E-TTL is greatly extended by the new cordless E-TTL control and by the high-speed-flash sync capability. But this flash unit offers a whole lot more. The guide number of 180 in feet (55 in meters) means that there is plenty of flash power for most applications. The flash automatically zooms to match the angle of view of the lens from 24mm to 105mm; a built-in wide-angle attachment extends this out to 17mm. The large LCD with light provides all operational information at a glance: flash mode, zoom position, lens aperture, flash range (switchable for feet or meters). "Flash ready" is indicated in two stages: first, the ready light glowing in green-yellow to indicate that a photo is possible but the capacitor is not yet fully charged; second, changing to red to indicate full charge. The flash confirmation light between the ready light and power switch comes on for about three seconds to indicate proper function and correct exposure. This is useful to monitor flash operation when the flash is at a remote location during cordless operation. Pressing the depth-of-field preview button when the flash is turned on causes the flash to produce a one-second burst of 70 rapid flash pulses at low power, which you can use to visualize the actual effect of the flash on your subject. This is great to help eliminate unwanted and unsightly shadows.

The Speedlite 550EX also has six of its own Custom Functions, which can be used to modify the flash to suit the individual photographer. You can, for example, change the order of bracketing in electronic flash bracketing, a very important function allowing you to take three photos with flash exposure bracketing (FEB). You can set these brackets on the flash up to +/–3 stops. Whether the increments are 1/3, 1/2, or full stops depends on how the camera is set. Because this function is integrated into the flash, it also works with some other EOS cameras, excluding the 600, 700 and 800 series. Second-curtain flash sync, stroboscopic effects, and some other effects are possible as well.

For those who find the 550EX either too heavy or too expensive, Canon also offers the 220EX and 380EX flash units. They have less power than the 550EX and offer fewer advanced features.

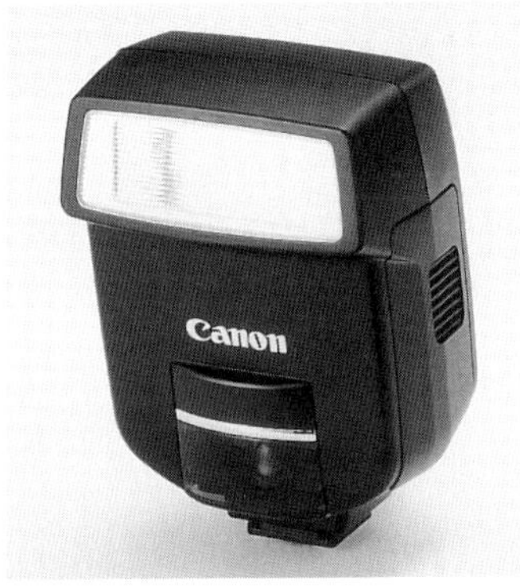

Canon Speedlite 220EX

Other Speedlites

While the 550EX is undoubtedly the best flash unit for use with the EOS-3, many long-time photographers may already own other Speedlite units. For the most part, these will also be compatible with the EOS-3 but will lack conveniences, such as E-TTL flash operation, cordless off-camera control, or high-speed-flash sync. Canon Speedlites 540EZ, 430EZ, 420EZ, or 300EZ will work very well on the EOS-3. Instead of E-TTL, they use A-TTL, which includes ambient light in flash exposure calculations but is less accurate. Rather than using a preflash like E-TTL, this system measures ambient exposure in three areas and the flash unit shuts off when proper flash exposure has been reached while the photo

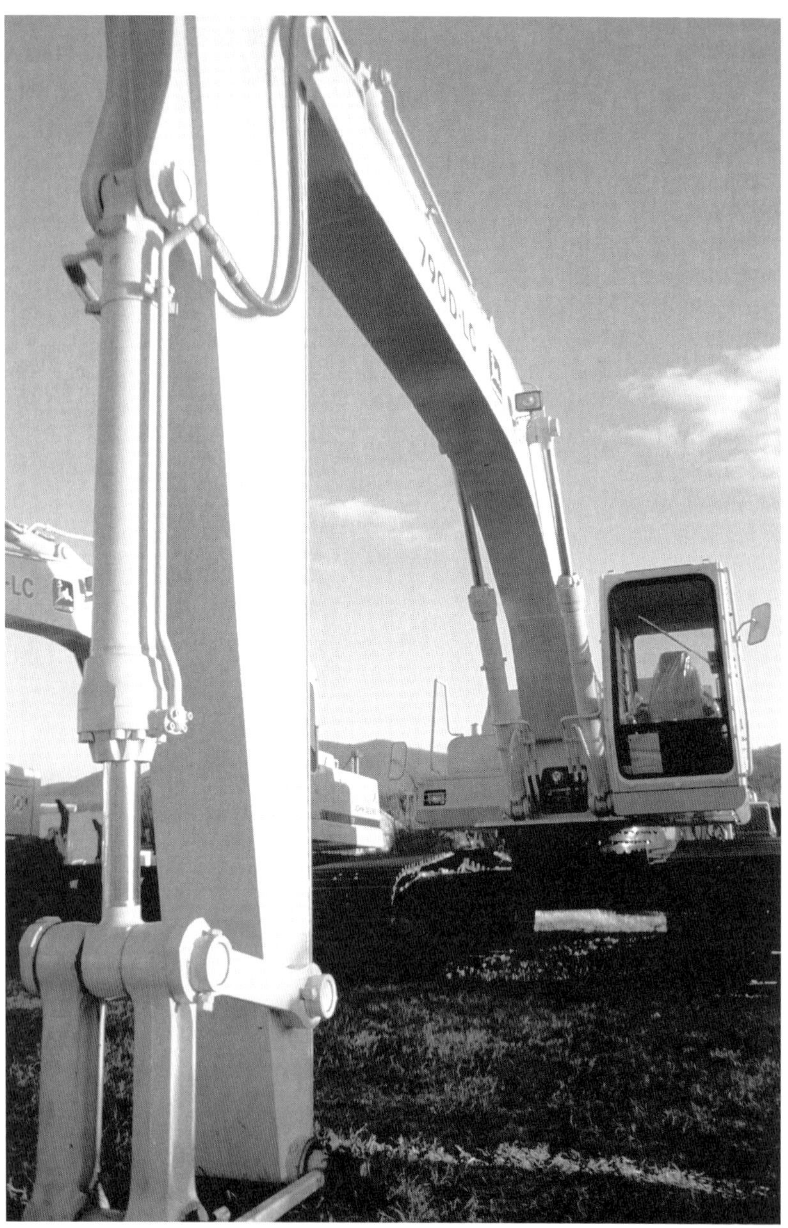
790D-LC

is being taken. This works well for balancing flash and ambient exposure but does not have the precision of E-TTL. These flash units, however, were the best available in their time—which was not so many years ago—and many photographers may find them still satisfactory for their needs.

Diffusers

Accessory manufacturers make numerous reflectors, diffusers, and other devices for use on hot-shoe flash units. They have a wide variety of shapes and sizes, and some even inflate. The idea in almost all cases is to soften the light by making the apparent size of the light source larger. For obvious reasons, they work best when the flash is mounted relatively close to the subject.

An image like this, which exhibits converging vertical lines and exaggerated perspective, requires you to get in close with a wide-angle lens. You can minimize that kind of distortion by taking the photo from a greater distance with a telephoto lens. Photo by Bob Shell.

Canon EF Lenses

A Brief History of Interchangeable Lenses

In its infancy, photography offered no distinctions among wide-angle, normal, and telephoto lenses. In 1890, the first photographic Galilean telescope, capable of magnifying a subject four times, was introduced. Only after Oskar Barnack invented small-format, 35mm photography, however, did it suddenly make sense to manufacture lenses with greatly varying focal lengths and fast apertures for photographic purposes.

In addition, along with the change from romantic photography to the new realism and the first successes of photojournalism came an increased demand for interchangeable lenses. In the 1960s, these lenses became standard in 35mm SLR cameras.

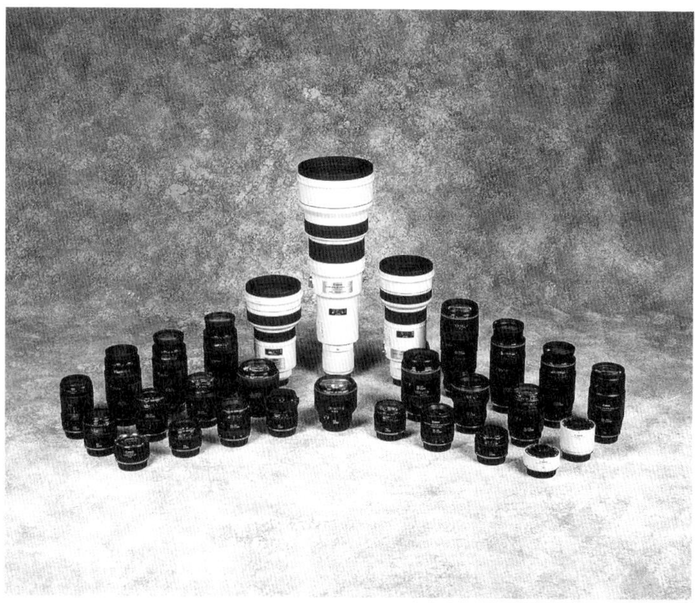

From extreme wide angles to extreme telephotos, Canon makes a lens to suit every photographic need. Photo by Heiner Henninges.

Canon's Contribution

Canon has always considered having its own complete line of lenses to be crucial to high-quality photography. It is not surprising, therefore, that pioneer efforts in this field are frequently connected with the Canon name—including technical equipment features that have become quality concepts in lens construction. For example, Canon has pioneered such ideas as internal focusing, lenses of calcium fluorite, aspherical lens surfaces (both ground and polished, and glass-molded aspherics), and most recently image stabilization (IS) lenses that can be used, handheld, at much slower shutter speeds.

The era of the Canon FD lenses ended with the introduction of the first EOS 650 in 1987. There were things that the Canon lens designers wanted to do that simply could not be done within the constraints imposed by the FD mount, primarily due to the relatively narrow diameter of the mount itself; certain high-speed lenses, for instance, required rear glass elements that were too large in diameter to fit into FD mounts. Canon realized that mechanical lens linkages were simply not accurate or durable enough for the lenses of the future.

The Canon EF Mount

The result of all of this was that Canon's engineers decided to

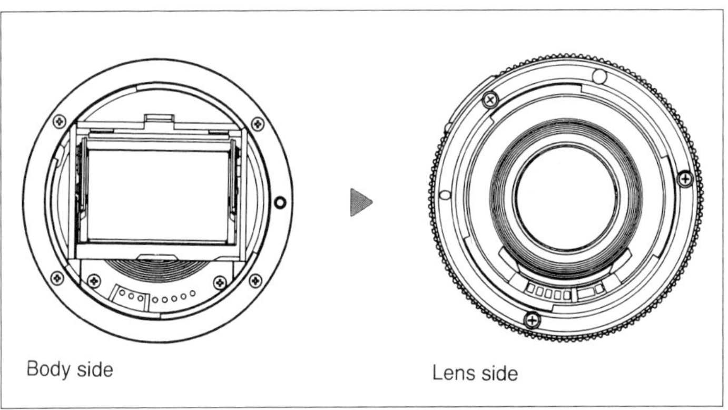

This drawing shows the lens bayonet mount of the camera (left) and the rear of the lens (right). Note the electrical contacts on both, which mate when the lens is mounted.

make a complete break with the FD mount tradition and introduce a totally new lens mount—the EF (electronic focus). The Canon EF mount is much larger in diameter, features a simple bayonet design, and has no mechanical linkages between the camera and the lens. Not only do the gold-plated electrical contacts convey information between the camera and the lens, they also carry the electrical power for the AF motor and the diaphragm motor, eliminating the need for a separate battery compartment in the lens. Canon engineers concluded early in their research that the AF motors belonged in the lenses, where the motors could be placed as close as possible to what they actually moved; in addition, each lens could be fitted with a motor best suited to its needs and specifications. This has resulted in the design of several different types of motors for EF lenses.

Arc Form Drive

The first type of motor Canon designed for EOS lenses was the Arc Form Drive (AFD). This is a very traditional small electrical motor whose components are arranged in an arc shape so that the motor fits easily into a lens barrel. While the AFD works very well, it wasn't quite fast enough for most applications, and it has been replaced with a new generation of motor. Because of special design considerations, however, one Canon EF lens—the 100mm f/2.8 macro, which has an exceptionally long extension—uses a traditional small electrical motor with a long drive shaft.

Ultrasonic Motors

The most advanced motor now being used is hardly a motor at all in the conventional sense of the word; it is simply two metal rings with special surfaces on their mating sides. These rings are held in contact by springs, one fixed in position while the other free to turn. An electrically excited piezoelectric crystal acts as an oscillator at ultrasonic frequencies to vibrate the rings. Because of the nature of their surfaces, the standing wave generated in the rings causes them to rotate against one another. Since one ring is fixed in place and the other one turns, the direction of rotation and speed of the turning ring are controlled by the frequency and intensity of the wave generated. Canon refers to this unusual device as an Ultrasonic Motor (USM).

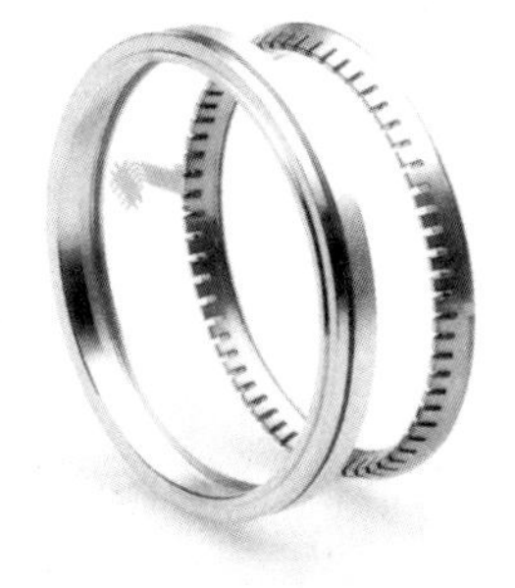

The ring-type USM motor uses high-frequency vibration to drive the lens. This motor is the fastest and quietest, but is expensive to manufacture.

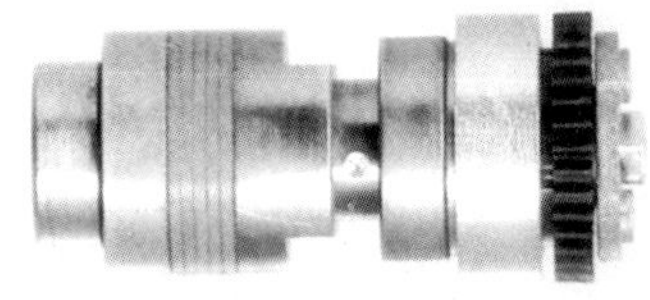

The newer Micro USM operates on the same principles, but is suited to mass production and is much less expensive. It is being used in place of AFD motors on all newer Canon AF lenses.

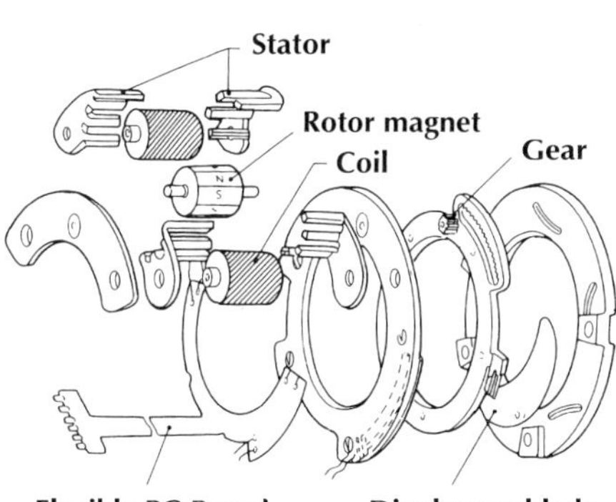

This diagram shows the construction of Canon's unique, electrically driven diaphragm mechanism, which uses stepper motors for precision and repeatability of aperture setting.

Initially, the manufacture of USMs was extremely expensive and quite complex; only relatively small numbers were built, and the first generation of USM (L-1) was used just for professional lenses. Continued research on USM technology has resulted in a total of three generations of USMs, each one designed to suit a specific purpose. The largest and most powerful is the L-1, a ring-type USM built into most Luxury (L-series) super-telephoto lenses and large-aperture lenses. Next is the M-1 (also a ring-type motor), which is used in a wide variety of consumer-level lenses. Unlike the L-1, which has an electronic manual focusing system, the M-1 USM has a less expensive mechanical manual focusing mechanism. The third generation is the Micro USM, introduced in 1992 with the EF 35-80mm f/4.0-5.6 USM. The Micro USM, which is not a ring-type motor, is used in Canon's entry-level EF lenses. It is faster and quieter than the DC Micro Motor it has replaced in many lenses.

The advantages of these special ultrasonic motors are many: they permit automatic focusing in almost all fields of professional photography; they do not have a clutch to prevent an immediate start, and thus are capable of a rapid response to even the most difficult automatic focusing problems; ring-type USM technology does not require the photographer to change settings on the lens for manual focusing; and, because an inaudible frequency of 29 to 31 KHz is responsible for the lenses' drives, USM lenses are virtually silent. This is a big plus when photographers do not wish to call attention to themselves.

Lens Designation and Performance

"EF mount" distinguishes every interchangeable lens that is compatible with Canon EOS system cameras. All of these lenses can be used on Canon's 35mm EOS SLRs, on Advanced Photo System EOS SLRs, and on VL-Mount interchangeable-lens camcorders (via an adapter). "L" identifies ultra-professional (Luxury) lenses, and "USM" indicates that a lens is focused by an Ultrasonic Motor. The abbreviation "TS-E" identifies tilt-and-shift lenses with electrical diaphragm operation, and "macro" indicates that a lens is specifically designed for the close-up range, allowing significant magnification. The latest addition to this letter code designation, IS, stands for image stabilization. This innovative technology uses a moving optical wedge and gyroscopes coupled to an electronic system to keep the image relatively stable even when the lens is not. In practice, this design is particularly useful when working from moving platforms, such as boats, and when taking photographs without a tripod or other support. With IS, I (Bob Shell) has found that I can handhold this lens, while bracing my body against a convenient support, at shutter speeds as slow as 1/8 second—unheard of when using a lens without IS technology. The practical development of IS is one of Canon's greatest technological breakthroughs, providing the photographer much greater freedom.

At the time the first EOS models appeared, 13 EF lenses were announced. Since then, many more EF lenses have been introduced. The high proportion of zoom lenses, covering focal lengths from 17mm to 400mm, is impressive. Almost a third of the zoom lenses and numerous fixed focal lengths in extreme performance ranges (L-series lenses) are of professional caliber. Canon's optical systems in general and the EF lenses in particular are so amazing that possible image aberrations and their causes need be given relatively little attention by the photographer.

The considerable challenge to optical engineers requires that they reduce aberrations appropriate to the problem to be solved by the lens, thus preventing residual aberrations—which occur even with proper use—from being conspicuous. Technical and scientific use and many professional applications require not only good quality, but the best quality, lenses. In these cases, it is important that maximum-performance quality of both lens and camera be noted with the "L" (Luxury) designation.

Lens Characteristics

Maximum Aperture

Maximum aperture (or lens speed) refers to the size of the largest opening (also called lens aperture) available on the lens; the aperture, which controls the amount of light that passes through the lens, works similarly to the iris of the eye. Apertures are expressed as f/stops, which are actually fractions. For example, f/16 is a smaller aperture than f/11 (think of it as the difference between 1/16 and 1/11); therefore, f/2.8 is a relatively large aperture, and an aperture of f/2 is larger yet. Opening the lens one full stop allows twice the amount of light to pass to the film. The amount of light is cut in half whenever the aperture is closed down to the next higher f/number (i.e., from f/11 to f/16).

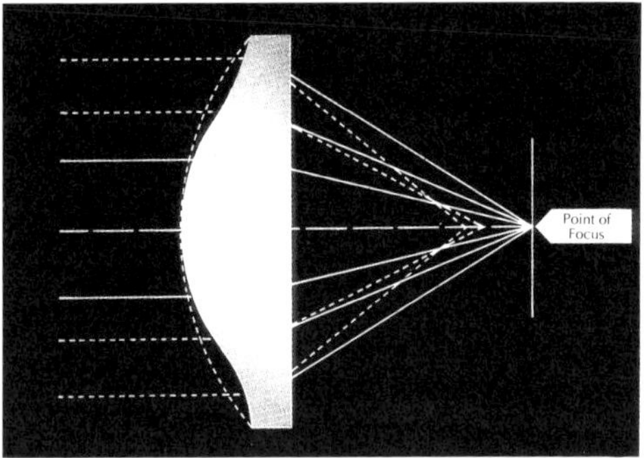

A normal, spherical lens (represented by dotted lines) focuses rays of light coming from the lens' outer edge at a point different from where rays passing through the center of the lens are focused. An aspherical lens corrects this so that all rays focus on the same plane.

Focal Length

Inside each lens assembly, light rays coming from infinity are bent so that they meet at a point of focus. The distance from the rear nodal point (optical center of the lens) to the film plane is defined as focal length. The angle of view covered by a lens is a function of focal length. A larger angle of view becomes a wide-angle lens, a small image angle becomes a telephoto lens, and a variable angle of view is characteristic of a zoom lens.

Focal length, usually considered the most important lens reference value, is indicated in millimeters and is independent of any film format.

Lens Care

Although the electrical contacts on the back of EF lenses are much less delicate than pins and levers, they still must be protected from environmental dust and dirt—and particularly from fingerprints—when the lens is not on the camera. The same goes for the rear glass of the lens, which is easily scratched. Always put a rear lens cap on a lens as soon as it is taken off the camera, and keep it there until just before the lens is again mounted onto the camera. Likewise, front lens caps should be left on all lenses when they are not in use.

If you do get dirt or dust onto the front or rear glass of the lens, you can remove it easily and safely. First, simply see if it will blow off. Camera dealers sell small squeeze-bulb blowers for this purpose, or you can buy an ear syringe from a drugstore. Gentle puffs of air will usually get rid of most dust and grit. If you encounter stubborn material, then you can use a brush, such as a soft camel's hair. Use this brush in a sweeping, circular pattern, starting at the center and working toward the edge of the lens. Hold the lens either sideways or with the glass surface to be cleaned, pointing downward so that gravity will carry away the offending matter. Then try the blower again.

If you still don't have success, take a lens-cleaning tissue or a special lens chamois and wipe gently, again in a circular motion, starting from the center. If even this does not work, moisten the tissue with a drop or two of lens cleaning fluid and try again, exerting only very gentle pressure. If none of these attempts work, take the lens to a professional.

Don't be a fanatic about dust, however. A few specks of dust on the front of your lens, a few on the rear, or even a few on the inside glass elements will not have a noticeable effect on your photos. Reasonable cleanliness is important, but do not cling to the idea that a single dust speck will ruin your photos.

Canon Lens Line

(Current as of date of publication)

Fixed Lenses

Canon EF 14mm f/2.8L USM
Canon EF 15mm f/2.8 Fisheye
Canon EF 20mm f/2.8 USM
Canon EF 24mm f/1.4L USM
Canon EF 24mm f/2.8
Canon TS-E 24mm f/3.5L
Canon EF 28mm f/1.8 USM
Canon EF 28mm f/2.8
Canon EF 35mm f/1.4L USM
Canon EF 35mm f/2.0
Canon TS-E 45mm f/2.8
Canon EF 50mm f/1.0L USM
Canon EF 50mm f/1.4 USM
Canon EF 50mm f/1.8 II
Canon EF 50mm f/2.5 Compact Macro

Canon EF 85mm f/1.2L USM
Canon EF 85mm f/1.8 USM
Canon TS-E 90mm f/2.8
Canon EF 100mm f/2.0 USM
Canon EF 100mm f/2.8 Macro
Canon EF 135mm f/2.0L USM
Canon EF 135mm f/2.8 with Soft Focus
Canon EF 180mm f/3.5L Macro USM
Canon EF 200mm f/1.8L USM
Canon EF 200mm f/2.8L II USM
Canon EF 300mm f/2.8L USM
Canon EF 300mm f/4.0L IS USM
Canon EF 300mm f/4.0L USM
Canon EF 400mm f/2.8L II USM
Canon EF 400mm f/5.6L USM
Canon EF 500mm f/4.5L USM
Canon EF 600mm f/4.0L USM
Canon EF 1200mm f/5.6L USM

Zoom Lenses
Canon EF 17-35mm f/2.8L USM
Canon EF 20-35mm f/3.5-4.5 USM
Canon EF 24-85mm f/3.5-4.5 USM
Canon EF 28-70mm f/2.8L USM
Canon EF 28-80mm f/3.5-5.6
Canon EF 28-80mm f/3.5-5.6 IV USM
Canon EF 28-105mm f/3.5-4.5 USM
Canon EF 28-135mm f/3.5-5.6 IS USM
Canon EF 22-55mm f/4.0-5.6 USM
Canon EF 35-80mm f/4.0-5.6 USM
Canon EF 35-80mm f/4.0-5.6 III
Canon EF 35-350mm f/3.5-5.6L USM
Canon EF 55-200mm f/4.5-5.6 USM
Canon EF 70-200mm f/2.8L USM
Canon EF 75-300mm f/4.0-5.6 IS USM
Canon EF 75-300mm f/4.0-5.6 II
Canon EF 75-300mm f/4.0-5.6 II USM
Canon EF 80-200mm f/4.5-5.6 II
Canon EF 100-300mm f/4.5-5.6 USM

Canon EF 100-300mm f/5.6L
Canon EF 100-400 f/4.5-5.6L IS USM

Extenders
Canon EF 1.4x
Canon EF 2x
Life-Size Converter EF

Three Lenses for the Beginner

The beginner is faced with a very difficult choice. With so many lenses to pick from and so many of them seemingly similar, how do you decide which lenses to buy? To start with, we recommend taking care to shop at a reputable photo dealer. Beware of bargain-priced camera outfits that are advertised something like, "Canon EOS-3 with three lenses, . . . only . . ." and at a ridiculously low price. The old rule applies: Know what you are buying and from whom you are buying it.

It used to be that most 35mm cameras were sold with a 50mm lens as a standard package. This was so much the case that the 50mm came to be known as the "normal" lens. Canon offers three different normal lenses for EOS cameras—the 50mm f/1.0L USM, the 50mm f/1.4 USM, and the 50mm f/1.8 II—and for some photographers any one of them would be the right choice. More often today, though, photographers are finding that they are happier with a "normal" zoom. Author Bob Shell's personal "normal" lens is the 28-80mm f/2.8-4.0L USM, which he has used for some years. It was an expensive lens, but it is incredibly sharp and replaces a minimum of three fixed lenses, the 28mm, 50mm, and 80mm.

Canon makes two separate series of EF lenses, which may be described as standard and super; the L (Luxury) series is Canon's top-of-the-line professional lens line. All of them have superlative performance characteristics, and all of them are expensive. But if your goal is to buy absolutely the best optics possible, nothing else can touch them. If money were no object, we would recommend you own three lenses: the 17-35mm f/2.8L USM, the 28-70mm f/2.8L USM, and the 100-300mm f/5.6L.

A more accessible three-lens kit would consist of the lower-priced 20-35mm f/3.5-4.5 USM, 28-135mm f/3.5-5.6 IS USM, and the standard 100-300mm f/4.5-5.6 USM. These lenses are all very good, and many professionals use them. In the case of the first two, the economical price is achieved by making them slower, but this also makes them smaller and lighter, which is an advantage. In the case of the 100-300mm, the difference is that the L uses exotic types of glass and has a higher degree of color correction.

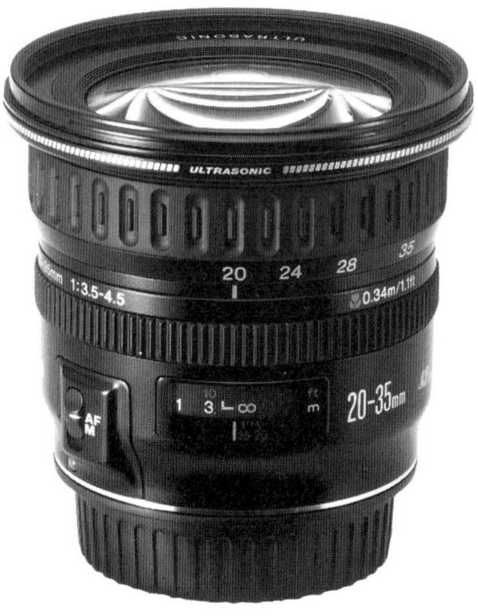

This 20-35mm variable-aperture wide-angle zoom lens is ideal for many applications, including interior photography and photojournalism.

Whether the slower and less expensive wide-angle and normal zooms, and the less expensive glass, will meet your needs depends entirely on the type of photography you do and your own critical standards. If you habitually work outdoors in bright light, they would certainly be adequate. If your forte is taking low-light photos in available light, then you would want the faster lenses and might bypass zooms altogether in favor of the very fast fixed-focal-length lenses. Or, if you do a lot of close-up work, one of the three macro lenses might make more sense to you. What *is* important is to know in advance what it is that you want to do photographically and then match the lenses you buy to the purpose. It makes no sense to buy a particular lens if you have no use for it just because it will impress people.

The point is that there are really no rules on which lens to use, only general guidelines. If a particular lens works for you for a particular picture, then it is the correct lens. What really matters behind all of this technical information about cameras and lenses is the final image. Ultimately, that is all that the viewer sees or cares about.

What follows is a discussion of a representative range of Canon EF lenses. For a more comprehensive discussion of Canon lenses, see *Magic Lantern Guide to Canon Lenses*.

Fisheye and Super-Wide-Angle Lenses

Fisheye lenses are examples of barrel distortion gone mad and totally uncorrected; the only straight lines that are rendered straight are those that pass through the exact center of the image. The days when an image taken with a fisheye lens brought gasps of astonishment to an audience are long gone. Everyone has seen the fisheye effect—far too much, in fact. This is not to say that we renounce all use of fisheye lenses, just that they should be used judiciously. Canon's 15mm f/2.8 fisheye for EOS cameras is one of the best of these special lenses.

Canon has chosen to make a full-frame fisheye, not one of the kind that produces a small circular image in the center of the film; instead, it fills up the frame and provides an approximately 180° view from corner to corner. This lens can be used to produce highly exaggerated perspectives in views of interiors, as well as for sweeping panoramas of landscapes in which the distortion is not obvious unless the lens is tilted up or down. George Lepp, the well-known nature photographer, tells us that he uses the fisheye for very close flower photos, sometimes getting all the way down on the ground and looking up at the flower from below. Don't be afraid to try unusual methods like this; the photos may be spectacular and certainly will get you thinking about ways to use unusual perspectives.

Though they are perhaps not as riveting as photos taken with fisheye lenses, photos taken with super-wide-angle lenses can still be remarkably striking. These lenses lend themselves to providing unusual perspectives and opening up spaces indoors as well as outdoors. In the category of super-wide-angle lenses, Canon has two lenses of fixed focal length and three zoom lenses: the EF 14mm f/2.8L USM, the EF 20mm f/2.8 USM, the EF 17-35mm f/2.8L USM, the EF 20-35mm f/3.5-4.5 USM, and the EF 22-55mm f/4.0-5.6 USM.

The fisheye design allows barrel distortion to go uncorrected—distorting straight lines into arcs as they become farther from the image center—while the 14mm is a rectilinear design with maximum correction for distortion. In other words, if aligned carefully, the 14mm lens will provide images with a minimum of barrel distortion. Any wide-angle lens will produce distortion if tilted up or down, but rectilinear ones will have very little if aligned carefully. For this purpose, an accessory bubble level that attaches to the camera hot shoe is a useful accessory, and is readily available from good photo shops.

One of the most important advantages of super-wide-angle lenses is that with them you can take in large areas from very short distances; this is particularly an advantage indoors in cramped surroundings. These lenses open up such surroundings, making them appear more spacious. Advertising photos of auto interiors are generally taken with wide-angle lenses for this reason; viewed through a 20mm, the cramped cockpit of a Lamborghini Diablo looks like the spacious interior of a limousine! Don't think that these lenses are just for indoors, however; they are also very useful out and about in the city. Just don't tip the lens up to get the tops of the buildings in—the exaggerated perspective of a super-wide-angle lens makes the buildings look as if they are falling down.

Canon EF 14mm f/2.8L USM: This super-wide-angle lens continues the old FD lens tradition and expands the previous maximum super-wide-angle range of 20mm down to a fabulous 14mm. The most amazing feature of the EF 14mm lens is the USM motor. Until now, Canon has preferred the AFD motor for the wide-angle range because the distance transfer could work with different shooting ranges and produce different effects; this allowed the photographer to fine-tune in the close-up range. If, however, the 20-35mm zoom is described as having fast AF adjustment, extremely fast must be used to describe this lens.

This super-wide angle exhibits surprisingly little vignetting (although some is still evident in this focal length range). Also,

Canon's EF 14mm f/2.8L USM is a very sharp, high-speed, super-wide-angle lens.

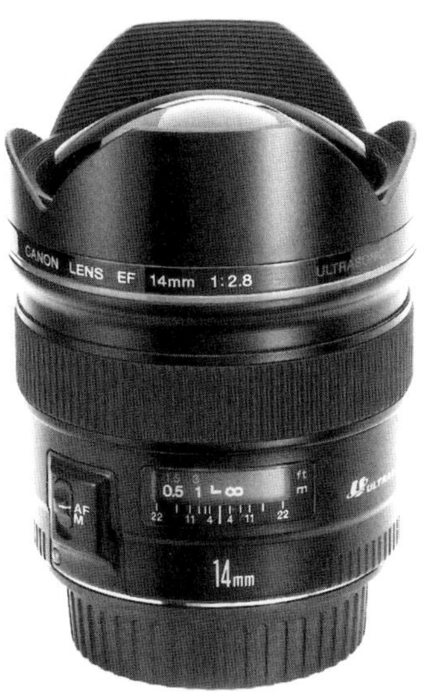

typical distortion is minor, thanks to the exceptional configuration of the optical system. Even though this system is based on the Canon FD 14mm lens, its optics have been redesigned completely. The second of the 14 elements in 10 groups is aspherical, which compensates for distortions along the edges. Astigmatism, which is particularly annoying at very short shooting distances, is neutralized by internal focusing; the distance between the front lens and the focusing element changes as the distance is changed. Instead of a genuine lens hood, these lenses have an abbreviated lens hood, which also acts as a front lens protector to prevent scratching of the domed front lens. The lens' construction allows the insertion of a gel filter in the optical path; there is no conventional filter mount. The Canon 14mm super-wide-angle lens can be used in an exceptionally effective way, especially with a reproduction scale of 1:10 and a shooting distance of 10 inches (25 cm). When the close-up setting and depth of field are used optimally, a sharp image over the entire range is produced.

The lens has a front lens diameter of 3 inches (7.7 cm) and a length of 3.5 inches (8.9 cm). Its smallest aperture is f/22. It weighs less than 20 ounces (560 g) and has an AF on/off switch to allow manual focusing.

The Canon EF 15mm f/2.8, a fisheye with a 180° angle of view.

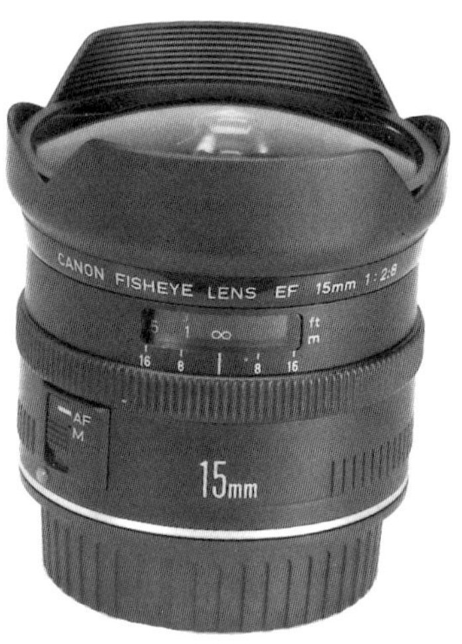

Canon EF 15mm f/2.8 Fisheye: The Canon EF fisheye focuses down to 8 inches (20 cm). This value does not represent the distance of the subject to the front of the lens but to the film plane. Due to this extreme perspective and the small scale of reproduction, this focal length features extreme depth of field, so it is not necessary to use the lens' smallest aperture of f/22 when everything in the picture—from a few inches to the horizon—is to appear sharp.

The built-in lens shade does not accommodate a standard screw-in filter. Therefore, the lens has a special snap-in filter mount. Filter gels, such as KODAK WRATTEN™ Filters, must be cut to 31 x 31 mm and inserted in the filter mount. From an optical point of view, it is of no consequence whether a filter is mounted in front of or within the lens.

In this lens, the optical system is comprised of eight elements in seven groups. The AFD focuses from infinity to 8 inches (20 cm) in exactly 0.36 second. The smallest subject area is 6.9 x 10.3 inches (17.1 x 25.7 cm). The lens length is 2.4 inches (6.2 cm), and the weight is 11.6 ounces (330 g).

Canon EF 20mm f/2.8 USM: This lens is completely different from the old FD-series 20mm f/2.8. It has a 94° angle of view, making it an excellent choice for showing more of a scene or for photographing in close quarters. It has a front lens diameter of

3.1 inches (7.75 cm) and a length of 3 inches (7.7 cm). Its smallest aperture is f/22, and it weighs less than 15 ounces (405 g). The minimum focusing distance is 10 inches (25 cm).

Canon EF 24mm f/2.8 and Canon EF 28mm f/2.8: Both of these lens types proved themselves in FD systems and were redesigned for EOS use. Whether the 24mm or the 28mm lens is the more sensible solution is mostly a question of preference.

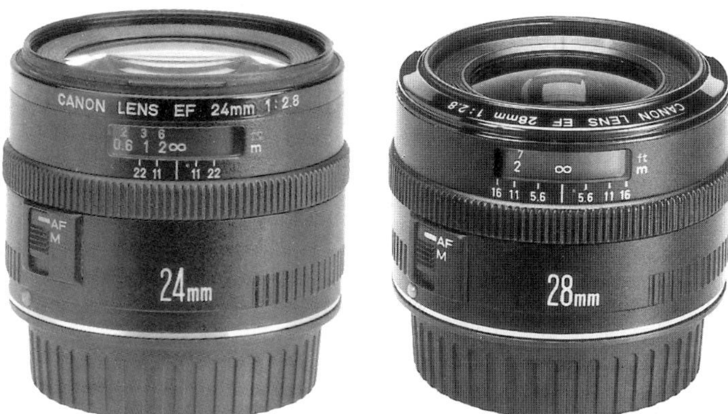

Canon's EF 24mm f/2.8 and EF 28mm f/2.8 lenses are ideal for shooting landscapes, architecture, interiors, and photojournalism.

The 24mm lens exhibits optimal correction at only 12 feet (4 m) because its engineers assumed that the sharpness in the infinity range is mostly a function of depth of field and rarely a result of direct adjustment. The lens has an image angle of 84°. At its shortest shooting distance, it produces an image size of 7.5 x 11.1 inches (18.5 x 27.7 cm). Because of floating elements, the close-up range of this lens offers high-quality image reproduction down to 10 inches (25 cm). Its focusing speed is 0.44 second from infinity to 10 inches (25 cm). The super-wide-angle lens has a length of about 2 inches (4.85 cm) and weighs only 9.5 ounces (270 g).

The 28mm has five elements in five groups, a minimum aperture of f/22, a filter size of 52mm, and an angle of view of 75°. At 1.7 inches (4.25 cm) long and 6.5 ounces (185 g) in weight, it produces high-quality reproduction down to a distance of 12 inches (30 cm).

Canon EF 28mm f/1.8 USM: This lens has an angle of view of 75° and a floating element design with 10 elements in nine groups. It has a minimum aperture of f/22, a filter size of 58mm, is 2.2 inches (5.6 cm) long, weighs 10.9 ounces (310 g), and is able to focus down to 10 inches (25 cm).

Normal Lenses

The most obvious advantages to normal lenses are their low weight and lens speed (wide maximum aperture). These lenses have a focal length that corresponds approximately to the size of the film diagonal, which in the 35mm format is about 43mm. Consequently, all the lenses within this class feature focal lengths between about 40mm and 60mm. A standard of 50mm has been preferred since the beginning of the 35mm era because of manufacturing and optical considerations.

Four lenses having a focal length of 50mm are available for the EOS-3 cameras and other EOS models, but only three are so-called "normal" lenses. The fourth is a macro lens with a particularly large close-up range (see page 165).

All four lenses have an angle of view of 46° across the diagonal. Image effects achieved with these lenses correspond more or less to the way the human eye sees the world. Even though zoom lenses within the normal lens range are used more and more frequently in place of fixed-focal-length lenses, fixed lenses still continue to be important.

Canon EF 50mm f/1.0L USM: Currently, this is the only AF standard 50mm focal length lens with a photographer's dream aperture of f/1.0. Its optical system includes two aspherical elements and special elements made of ultra-low-dispersion (UD) glass with a high index of refraction. The main advantage of this optical system is high-quality optics with a very large aperture. The lens is one stop faster than the 50mm f/1.4 lens.

The 50mm f/1.0 focuses down to 24 inches (60 cm). When shooting objects at a distance—a street scene, for instance—the lens' focusing range can be limited. This allows the system to focus more rapidly in a shorter, usable range. Focusing the long distance from infinity to 24 inches (60 cm) takes exactly one second.

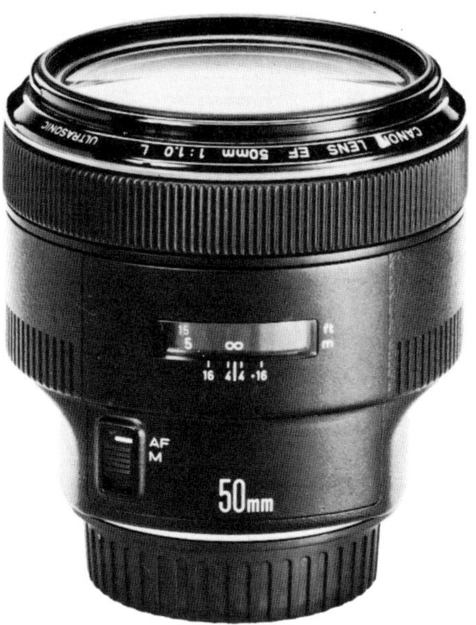

The EF 50mm f/1.0L is an unusually fast specialty lens designed for low-light photography.

A maximum aperture of f/1.0 certainly is not a requirement for everybody, but those who shoot subjects in difficult lighting conditions will be aided by this lens. The depth of field with an aperture of f/1.0 and a shooting distance of exactly 24 inches (60 cm) begins at 23.4 inches (59.5 cm) and ends at 23.7 inches (60.3 cm).

The lens system consists of 11 elements in nine groups, having a total weight of just over 35 ounces (985 g). The lens has a length of 3.2 inches (8.1 cm), a maximum diameter of 3.6 inches (9.1 cm), and a filter size of 72mm. The smallest subject area (reproduction ratio 1:11) is 8.9 x 13.4 inches (22.8 x 34.2 cm).

Canon EF 50mm f/1.4 USM: With a maximum aperture of f/1.4, this lens is a half stop faster than the 50mm f/1.8 lens. It is well suited for taking pictures at the theater or circus, as well as in museums, churches, or other places with low light; with high-speed film, in fact, there may not even be a need for flash. This lens, which provides a very bright viewfinder image, high resolution, high contrast, and excellent color balance, has capabilities not even remotely met by many standard zoom lenses, and its performance is exceptional, even at full aperture.

Comprised of seven elements in six groups, and with a close-up limit of 18 inches (45 cm), the lens has a length of 2.9 inches (7.4 cm) and weighs only 10.1 ounces (290 g). Thanks to its micro USM, this lens can focus extremely quickly, making practically no sound. It also allows manual adjustment without deactivating the AF function.

Canon EF 50mm f/1.8 II: The difference in maximum aperture between a small zoom lens and this fixed lens is almost two stops—a significant difference between the EF 50mm f/1.8 and zoom lenses with this focal length! This normal lens focuses as close as 18 inches (45 cm) and covers a reproduction scale of 1:15.

The optical system consists of six elements in five groups. The lens has a DC Micro Motor for automatic focus and can be focused manually as well. The drive speed from infinity to its closest focusing distance, 18 inches (95 cm), is 0.27 second; the lens can be closed to an aperture of f/22; and the filter diameter is 52mm. The front ring does not rotate during focusing, which is important when using polarizing and special-effect filters. The standard lens has a length of only 1.6 inches (4.1 cm) and weighs under 5 ounces (130 g).

Short Telephoto Lenses

Short telephoto lenses, those in the general range from 70mm up to about 150mm, are often called portrait lenses. Giving them such a label is unnecessarily limiting, though, as they are useful for a large number of subjects other than portraits. The EOS line currently boasts five fixed lenses that fit into this range, and 16 zoom lenses! You certainly have plenty to choose from here.

Short telephoto lenses are really well suited to portraits only from the range of about 70mm up to about 150mm, because they both force the photographer to think in terms of head-and-shoulders shots, and provide a very undistorted and flattering perspective for the portrait subject. Ideal working distance is maintained ranging from about 3 feet (1 m) at one extreme to about 12 feet (3.7 m) at the other.

Typically, these lenses are used for portraiture at wide apertures to throw backgrounds and foregrounds out of focus and place all emphasis on the subject. You should never let this labeling of short telephotos as portrait lenses persuade you, however, not to use other lenses for portraits. I (Bob Shell) have often taken portrait photos with lenses in the 180mm to 200mm range, and know a professional glamour photographer in New York who normally takes head-and-shoulders portraits with 300mm and 400mm lenses because he likes the perspective better; his photos grace the covers of major magazines around the world, so others must agree. I have been in his studio during a session, and he is so far away from the model that he has to shout directions to her!

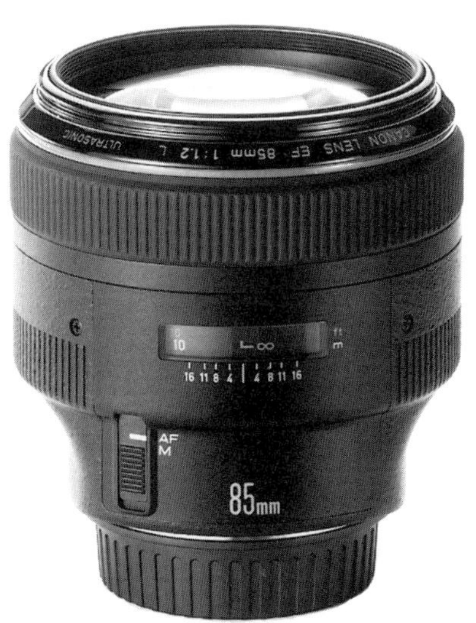

Canon EF 85mm f/1.2L USM

Canon EF 85mm f/1.2L USM: This ultra-fast telephoto lens has a length of just 3.3 inches (8.4 cm), a diameter of 3.6 inches (9.15 cm), and weighs 36 ounces (1025 g). Together with the EOS-3, this lens fits nicely in the hand, allowing any photojournalist to shoot at 1/30 second with a wide aperture and without a tripod. The ultrasonic motor makes almost no sound. The viewfinder image appears extremely bright due to the lens' high speed of f/1.2. This lens will become the personal standard lens for many quality fanatics.

An aspherical element assures that the aperture of f/1.2 will not be a novelty, but will truly deliver the professional quality expected. Considering its characteristics, this lens will be cherished by many photographers. Although it belongs to the family of lenses with long focal lengths, it does not compress the linear perspective and does not cause conspicuous spatial restriction. It is most suitable for normal-perspective shots and offers the additional advantage of a slightly smaller imaging field (compared with a 50mm focal length). The scale of reproduction is enlarged by a factor of 1.7. This is a very pleasant ratio for portrait, landscape, and action shots. Large apertures allow the photographer to determine the depth of focus precisely, desirable for portrait and landscape shots.

The super-fast portrait telephoto lens system consists of eight elements in seven groups, including an aspherical lens. The design uses additional floating elements to ensure high reproduction quality at all shooting distances. The image angle is 28°30´. The high-speed ultrasonic motor runs the extremely long focusing path from infinity to only 38 inches (95 cm) in just 1.2 seconds. Manual focus is possible at any time. The smallest subject area is 9 x 13.6 inches (22.8 x 34.5 cm).

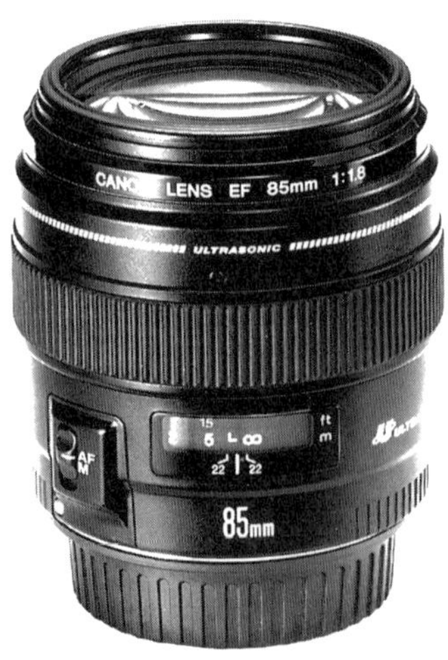

Canon EF 85mm f/1.8 USM

Canon EF 85mm f/1.8 USM: For those on a more restricted budget, the 85mm f/1.8 USM is more practical than the 85mm L lens. It delivers excellent quality in both contrast and sharpness with nine elements in seven groups, a minimum aperture of f/22, a minimum focusing distance of 33.5 inches (85 cm), and an angle of view of 28°30´. Its filter size is 58mm, its length is 2.9 inches (7.5 cm), and it weighs 14.9 ounces (425 g)—in all, very similar to the EF 100mm f/2.0 USM in size, weight, and cost.

Canon EF 100mm f/2.0 USM: The maximum aperture of f/2 can produce high-quality pictures at light levels where photographers with zoom lenses have long since given up. The fastest aperture a zoom lens can deliver at the 100mm focal length is only f/4.5 to f/5.6—a difference of 2 to 2-1/2 stops when compared to the 100mm f/2.0. Even after the photographer with a zoom has reached a shutter speed of 1/30 second, comfortable handheld shots can be taken of the same subject with this lens at 1/200 to 1/180 second. Also, the viewfinder image is brighter by the same factor.

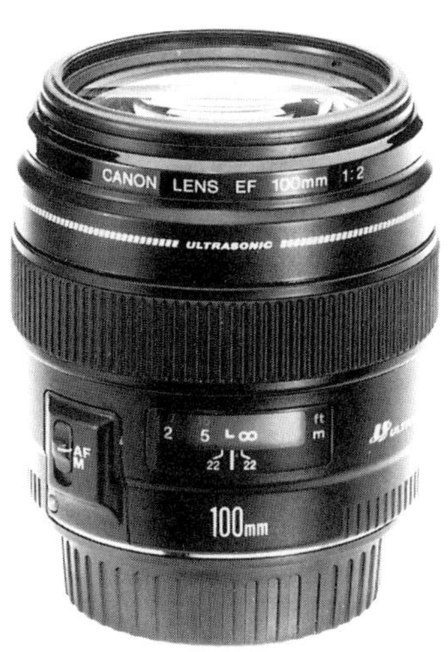

Canon EF 100mm f/2.0 USM

The quality in the close-up range is very high. In addition, this lens offers good image reproduction with a fully open aperture and is ideal for landscapes and portraits; even normal snapshots made in difficult lighting situations can be handled comfortably. The new USM motor, with optional manual adjustment and the internal focusing feature, allows lightning-fast focusing over the entire range within 0.4 second. The image angle is 24°.

The eight lens elements in five groups assure sharpness. The lens barrel does not change in length during focusing, providing optimum balance, and a photographer using a polarizing filter will welcome the fact that the front ring does not turn during focusing. At a length of 2.9 inches (7.35 cm), a weight of 16.1 ounces (460 g), and a size of 56mm, the lens fits comfortably in the hand. The lens hood (ET-65II) should always be attached.

Canon EF 200mm f/2.8L II USM: The advantages offered by this high-speed telephoto lens are selective sharpness and sharp focus; the close-up limit is 4.9 feet (1.5 m). The lens system consists of nine elements in seven groups, with two lenses of UD glass exhibiting anomalous dispersion characteristics. These lenses reduce color errors and ensure high-contrast sharpness.

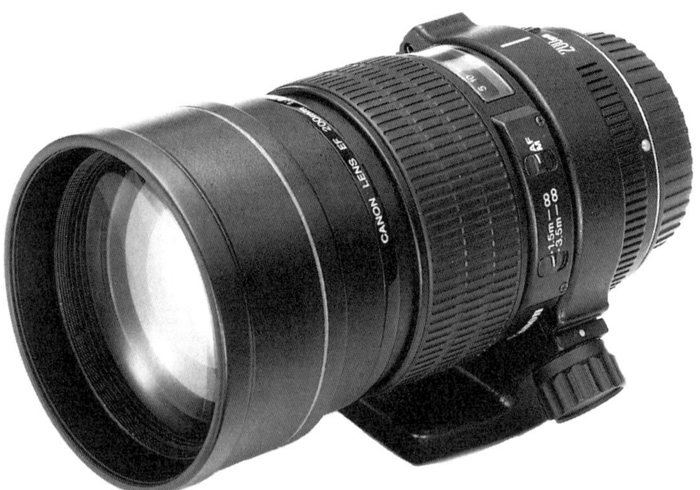

Canon EF 200mm f/2.8L II USM

The lens' 12° angle of view offers an impressive perspective, in the close-up range in particular. The lens has a length of 5.4 inches (13.6 cm) and weighs 1.7 pounds (0.8 kg).

It would be a pity not to use this lens with a Canon extender (1.4x or 2x) to make it an AF USM lens featuring values of 280mm f/4 or 400mm f/5.6. In both cases, the close-up limit is 4.9 feet (1.5 m).

Super Telephoto Lenses

Canon EF 300mm f/4.0L USM: This lens is a less expensive alternative to the EF 300mm f/2.8L. In many respects, it is comparable to the EF 200mm f/2.8L. Its exterior is similar to the large, gray super lenses, and rightfully so, because it carries the L in its name and hence may be considered to be Canon lens nobility. It has two UD glass elements, which reduce imaging errors to a minimum. Canon EF 1.4x and 2x extenders can be

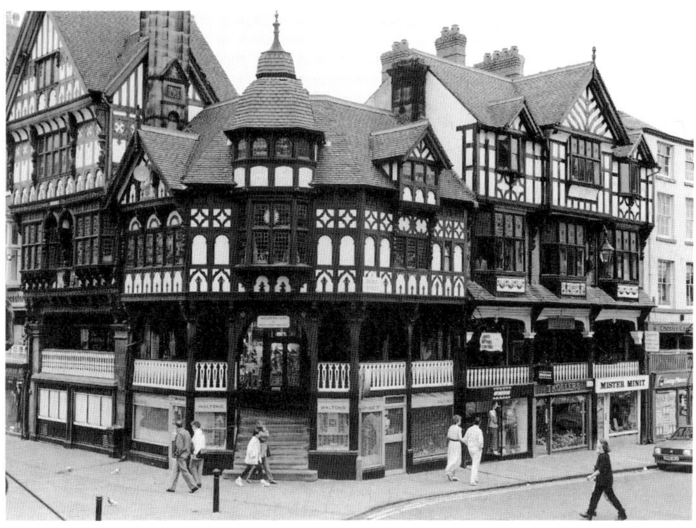

The geometric patterns of a Tudor building in Manchester, England, are even more striking when captured on black-and-white film. Photo by Bob Shell.

used, making it into a 420mm f/5.6 or 600mm f/8 lens, respectively. Autofocus is possible when the 1.4x extender is used with this lens; if used with the 2x extender, however, the lens must be focused manually.

The close-up shooting distance is 8.2 feet (2.5 m), resulting in a scale of reproduction of 1:7.7. Nine elements in seven groups make up the lens, giving it a length of 8.37 inches (21.3 cm) and a diameter of 3.6 inches (9.1 cm), covering an angle of view of 8°15´. Its image sharpness and excellent contrast are impressive.

More recently, a new version of this lens, integrating Canon's remarkable IS technology, has been introduced.

Canon EF 400mm f/5.6L USM: This super telephoto is the alternative to the 400mm f/2.8L II USM lens, which costs considerably more. Two low-dispersion UD elements minimize chromatic aberration. For the first time, a newly developed type of glass was used that exhibits even less light scatter, as well as characteristics that are normally achieved only by using sensitive fluorite crystals.

The fastest AF setting of this lens' M-1 USM covers two focal ranges. For shorter focusing times, the photographer can restrict the distance range from 11.5 feet (3.5 m) to infinity to 27.9 feet (8.5 m) to infinity. An extender can be used, but the focus must be set manually to accommodate the small maximum aperture.

The lens has a length of 10.1 inches (25.6 cm), a filter size of 77mm, and a weight of 2.7 pounds (1.25 kg), making it a lightweight in its class. Even though the tripod mount can be removed for handheld shots, the use of a tripod (or at least a monopod) is recommended whenever this lens is used.

Canon EF 500mm f/4.5L USM: This powerful telephoto lens is particularly lightweight and compact. Despite its large maximum aperture of f/4.5, its weight could be maintained at 6.6 pounds (3 kg)—keeping its weight at half as much as the EF 400mm f/2.8L II USM. By using lenses of synthetic crystalline fluorite and glass exhibiting an extremely low index of refraction, residual chromatic aberration errors have been almost eliminated. In addition, both sharpness and color reproduction have been improved significantly. The ultrasonic drive, along with the internal focusing system, ensures fast focusing; its minimum focusing

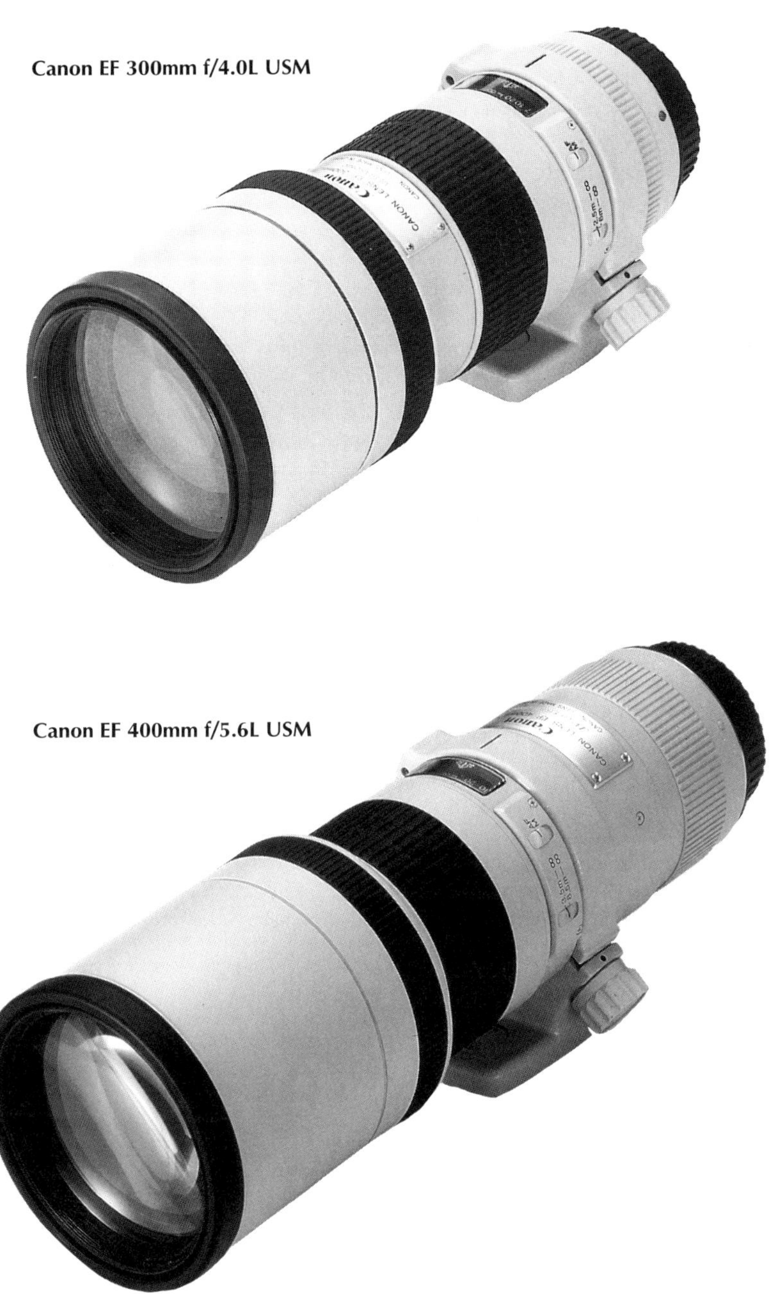

Canon EF 300mm f/4.0L USM

Canon EF 400mm f/5.6L USM

distance is 16.4 feet (5 m). A filter drawer holds 48mm filters; gelatin filters with filter holders can also be used. The lens has a length of 15.4 inches (39 cm) and a maximum diameter of 5.2 inches (13.2 cm). The optical system consists of seven elements in six groups.

Fast Telephoto Lenses

Canon's powerful giants for professional applications are the optical treats of the EF interchangeable lens program. All of them have a large metal lens hood, a stable foot with a rotating mechanism and tripod thread mount, and loops for a carrying strap. The smallest weighs 6.3 pounds (2.9 kg), the largest (1200mm f/5.6L USM), 36.3 pounds (16.5 kg). Even though they all belong to one family, each lens has its own special features. Altogether, they are dream lenses for anyone whose job requires work with such long focal lengths and for those who simply want to indulge themselves.

Fluorite and UD lens elements ensure top ratings for contrast and resolution. These special lenses are easy to handle, and all of them allow the photographer to store a preset shooting distance. It does not matter how many times other distances have been measured—a slight turn of the focusing ring and the lens is reset to the stored value. (The presetting mechanism has an optional, audible confirmation signal.) Sports photographers will really appreciate this distance preset feature. In fractions of a second, faster than the camera can be redirected at the subject, the photographer can continue to take pictures in the second preset distance range.

The ultrasonic motor offers electronic support for manual focusing. When the focusing ring is rotated, electrical pulses are generated, which signals to the lens' microprocessor that the ultrasonic motor should run. In this way, manual focusing causes almost no vibrations. All of these lenses feature adjustable manual focusing speeds (low, medium, and high) to suit the subject. They also offer the photographer the option of adapting the manual adjustment to his or her liking. Step 1 (low) offers half the rate of rotation, which is very useful for portraits or subjects in the close-up range and wherever very precise adjustment is important. Step 2 (medium) uses the normal rate of rotation, and Step 3

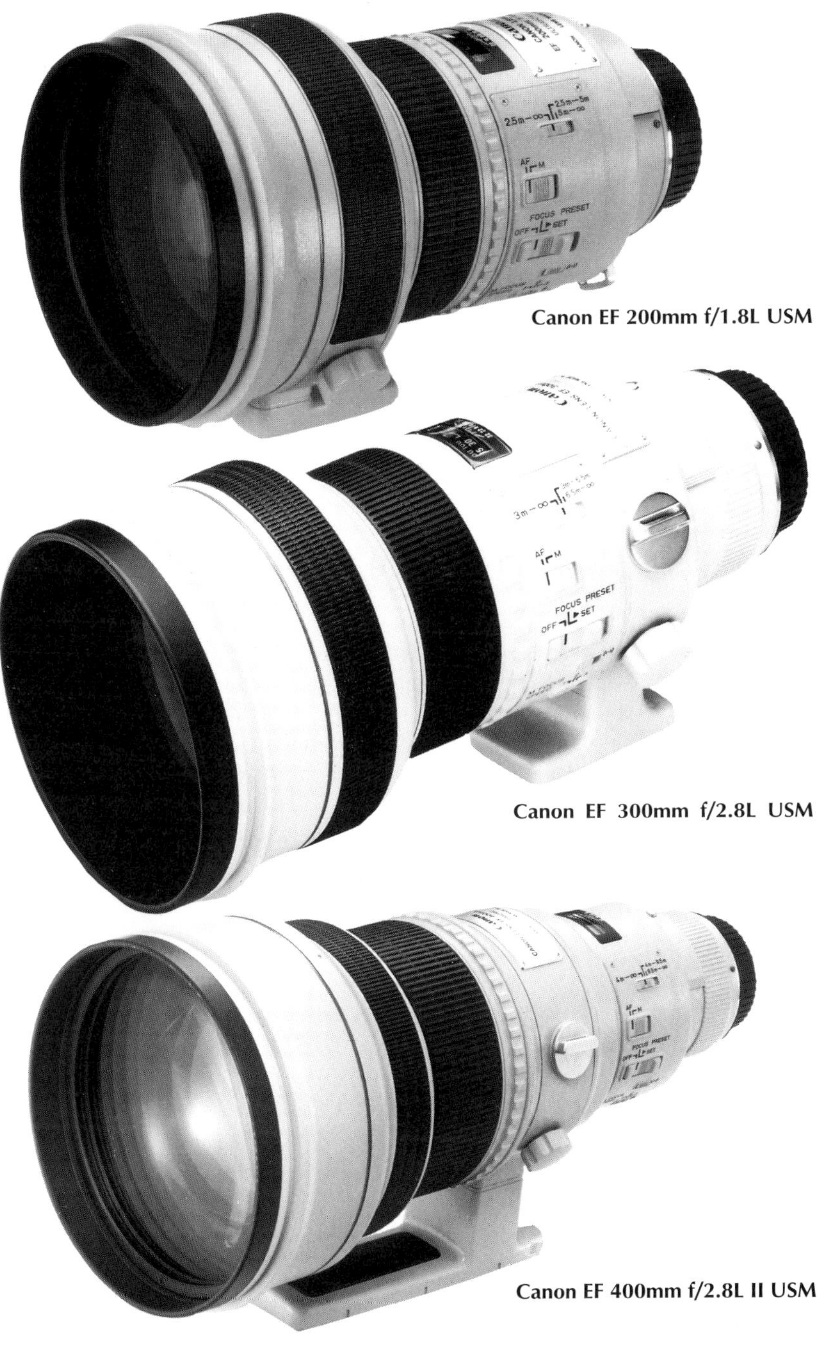

Canon EF 200mm f/1.8L USM

Canon EF 300mm f/2.8L USM

Canon EF 400mm f/2.8L II USM

(high) uses double the rate of rotation, as is frequently required in sports photography.

The telephoto lens' focusing paths are normally relatively long; therefore, these four Canon lenses, described below, have preset focusing ranges to shorten the adjustment process whenever possible. A slip-in filter mount permits the use of filters with these lenses. Normal Canon screw-mount filters in 48mm size, or even a circular polarizing filter of the same size, can be attached. A special gel filter holder accessory is available. Because all lenses are apochromatically corrected, they do not require refocusing when used with infrared film.

The use of a tripod with these lenses is absolutely essential to receive the best quality image. A stable monopod is recommended if more camera mobility is required, as when taking sports shots.

Canon EF 300mm f/2.8L USM: As far as the optics are concerned, this lens is the successor of the FD 300mm f/2.8L, which has many devotees among sports photographers. The AF model was the world's first lens with the USM drive, and still the star today at football stadiums and playing fields. Many professionals consider this lens the standard in terms of quality, speed, and price. Because the quiet USM drive does the focusing, this lens is as suitable for stage and theater photographers as it is for wildlife, landscape, sports, and press photographers. It is great as well for big-time media events, when photographers could be exiled to ditches or behind barriers. With the Canon extenders, focal lengths of 420mm or 600mm at f/4 or f/5.6 are achieved. This lens produces a 6x magnification and, in combination with extenders, an 8.5x or 12x magnification compared to a 50mm normal lens. One calcium fluorite element and one UD glass element provide optical correction for unsurpassed sharpness at great distances, along with exceptional color saturation.

Canon EF 400mm f/2.8L II USM: In 1980, when Canon introduced the first FD 400mm f/2.8 lens, it became the immediate rage among sports photographers. Now this AF 400mm lens shines as the current star. The entire focusing range from infinity to 13.2 feet (4 m) can be run in only 0.7 second. Two UD glass elements ensure professional sharpness, as expected from this

L-series lens. Extenders make it into a 560mm f/4.0 or a 800mm f/5.6. At a length of barely 14 inches (35 cm), it is surprisingly compact and exceptionally suitable for all subjects, including landscape, sports, action, and wildlife photography.

The optical system consists of 11 elements in nine groups. The diagonal image angle is 6°10´; rapid internal focusing is ensured by the USM drive. The lens weighs 13 pounds (5.9 kg) and has a length of 13.7 inches (34.8 cm). Its largest diameter is 6.6 inches (16.7 cm).

Canon EF 600mm f/4.0L USM: Wildlife, sports, and fashion photographers use this lens regularly. Two UD glass elements with anomalous partial dispersion and a calcium fluorite element with a large diameter were required to eliminate the secondary spectrum to allow this lens to equal other L-series lenses in its quality and performance.

A 1.4x extender makes the 600mm f/4.0 lens into an 800mm f/5.6 lens. By using the 2x extender, it is possible to convert this lens into a 1200mm f/8 super-telephoto lens—which, however, must be focused manually. Other than that, rapid focusing is ensured by the USM drive and the rear-component focusing system. A focus-preset function allows a lightning-fast change to a preselected focal setting. The manual focusing ring has a motor-assist device.

The optical system consists of nine elements in eight groups. The image angle is 4°10´ and the shortest shooting distance is at 19.7 feet (6 m). The super telephoto lens weighs 13.2 pounds (6 kg), has a length of 18 inches (45.6 cm), and a maximum diameter of 6.6 inches (16.7 cm).

Canon EF 1200 f/5.6L USM: This lens, manufactured only by special order, has the greatest focal length of any AF lens, and a price to match. As you can imagine, they aren't purchased often; they can be rented by accredited press photographers at large sports events. The data on this lens is quite impressive. Its optical system consists of 13 elements in 10 groups. Two fluorite lenses eliminate chromatic aberration and ensure a sharp image at maximum aperture.

Three focal ranges can be preselected for the shortest focusing periods, aided by the fast, super-quiet ultrasonic motor. With an

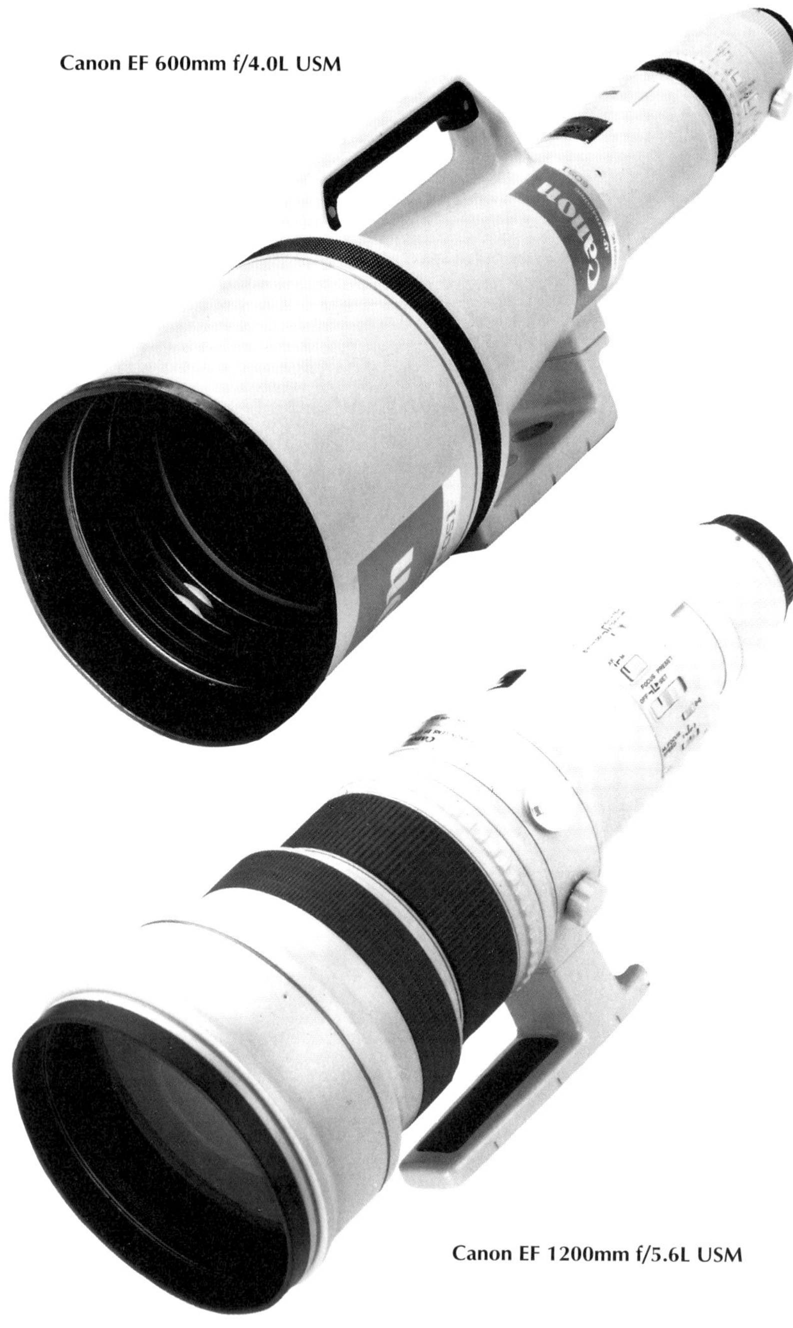

Canon EF 600mm f/4.0L USM

Canon EF 1200mm f/5.6L USM

image field of 10.8 x 16.3 inches (27.5 x 41.3 cm), the first range covers from 46 feet (14 m) to 98.4 feet (30 m). The second full focal range covers 46 feet (14 m) to infinity, and the third from 98.4 feet (30 m) to infinity. The lens has a length of 33 inches (83.8 cm), a weight of 36.3 pounds (16.5 kg), and a diameter of 9.2 inches (23.4 cm). The lens barrel, with a diameter of 48mm, is designed to hold insertable filters. A handle allows a quick switch between landscape and portrait formats.

It is even possible to use Canon extenders on this monster lens. An EF 1.4x makes this lens into a 1700mm f/8 super-telephoto lens, and an EF 2x into a 2400mm f/11 lens—allowing shots of details of the moon. The maximum aperture, f/11, requires manual focus.

Zoom Lenses

There are many photographers who simply refuse to use zoom lenses at all because they cling to the prejudice that zoom lenses do not produce sharp images. Zoom lenses got this reputation in their early days, and the first zoom lenses, such as the Voigtlander Zoomar, were pretty bad by any standard. But that was many years ago, and much technological progress has been made during those years. Early on, Canon discovered a relatively simple design principle for zoom lenses. This is why inexpensive zoom lenses that exhibit high quality and retain a small size are now available. Today, we have high-quality zoom lenses that give very little away to fixed focal length lenses.

As do fixed focal length lenses, zoom lenses have their advantages, and most well-equipped photographers will have some of both types for use in different circumstances. For example, even though I (Bob Shell) usually use the 28-80mm f/2.8-4.0L USM zoom, I also have the 85mm f/1.8 USM. Why? Because at the 80mm end of its zoom range, the 28-80 becomes f/4.0, and that is not fast enough for some purposes. Also, it does not allow me to set a really shallow depth of field, as I can easily do with the 85mm by simply setting it to f/1.8 or so. For a similar reason, I also have a 50mm f/1.8, although I do not use it very much. But when you need it, nothing else will do. (Lenses mentioned in this paragraph may have been discontinued.)

When taking photos with a zoom lens, we recommend that you adjust it first to its greatest focal length. As soon as the camera is placed up to your eye and the viewfinder image is in focus, the best possible image has usually been achieved. Candids are optimally shot right away; then, the image angle can be changed to determine whether the image might be framed better. A better frame happens relatively rarely, however, and if it does it's frequently at the other end of the focal length range. When you shorten the focal length, the distance setting is changed only in rare cases; this happens more frequently when you work the other way around.

In many situations, for example when you're going on a trip or whenever you do not want to carry additional lenses, a focal length range of 35mm to 105mm—or even 135mm—is ideal. This means that not only can you shoot subjects at the desired reproduction scale with a single lens, but you can also be creative with the focal length.

The wide-angle range offers a more panoramic view of a landscape, allows a large group of people to be in one picture, and helps solve restrictive or crowded spatial conditions in indoor shots.

The focal length range, between 80mm and 100mm, is ideal for taking photos of people and snapshots at parties and sporting events. Wide angles used to take landscapes produce pictures that exhibit a more neutral perspective; due to their slight telephoto effect, however, they ensure that the selected image frame does not appear overloaded. All in all, this is a universal focal length range.

Almost all zoom lenses have a so-called "macro" (close-up) setting. This setting is no substitute, however, for a macro lens, which is designed especially for extreme close-up work. A zoom lens' macro setting relies on the sharpness it achieves at the center of the lens, and therefore requires that you set a small aperture to obtain sufficient depth of field. The apparently reduced distance setting represents the actual working range of the lens and should always be set just to prevent unnecessary focusing adjustments. The shortest focusing distance setting for any zoom lens is the lens' macro setting, and the normal AF range is from that value to infinity.

Canon EF 20-35mm f/3.5-4.5 USM: For years, Canon has offered a professional-quality lens using this focal length range. The 20-35mm super-wide-angle zoom lens, with a maximum aperture of f/3.5 to 4.5, is a surprisingly good-quality lens at an affordable price.

Distortions may become a problem, in particular in the super-wide-angle zoom range. By consistently using spherical elements, Canon has significantly minimized these difficulties and achieved high resolution with only insignificant distortions along the image edges. In addition, a type of diaphragm blocks flare, which would ordinarily impair contrast.

The minimum shooting distance is 13.5 inches (34 cm). The lens system consists of 12 elements in 11 groups and features internal focusing. The front lens does not rotate, and filters with a diameter of 77mm as well as polarizing filters can be used in the super-wide-angle range. As is the case with other lenses, a lens hood (EW-83) should be used at all times.

Canon EF 22-55mm f/4-5.6 USM: This new lens is a very unusual focal length range, going from very wide to normal. It uses nine elements in nine groups, one element a replica aspheric. The lens focuses down to 13.7 inches (3.5 cm), accepts 58mm filters, and measures 2.6 x 2.3 inches (6.6 x 6 cm). It is also very light at only 6.2 ounces (175 g).

Canon EF 24-85mm f/3.5-4.5 USM: This versatile lens offers the photographer a wide range of focal lengths, from wide-angle to short telephoto. Its ring-type USM delivers nearly silent operation and quick AF response. The lens features on-demand manual focus; there is no M/AF switch. It close-focuses to 19.6 inches (50 cm), has 15 elements in 12 groups, is 2.87 inches (6.9 cm) long, and weighs 13.3 ounces (380 g).

Canon EF 28-80mm f/3.5-5.6 IV USM: This zoom lens, which has become the new standard lens in the zoom range, illustrates Canon's revised basic conception of the EOS system. Improved USM technology and the development of a micro USM for mass production integrate the advantages of this AF drive system in less expensive EF lenses. The 28-80mm lens features lead-free glass elements and a fixed auxiliary diaphragm (a baffle) between the second and third zooming groups, which acts to suppress flare throughout the entire focal length range. All of these features ensure that this zoom lens provides surprising quality at a favorable price.

The optical system, which consists of 10 elements in 10 groups, can focus as close as 15 inches (38 cm). It has a length of 2.8 inches (7.1 cm) and a maximum diameter of 2.6 inches (6.6 cm). Depending on the set focal length, the smallest aperture varies from f/22 to f/38. The filter size is 58mm. This zoom lens weighs 7.1 ounces (200 g).

Canon EF 28-80mm f/3.5-5.6: This lens is similar to the more expensive 28-80mm USM version. With its DC Micro Motor, however, it is a touch slower and not quite as quiet. These concessions, though, do not affect the quality of picture it takes and are worth the savings to the cost-conscious photographer.

Canon EF 28-105mm f/3.5-4.5 USM: This is an excellent zoom with highly corrected optics and a wide range of focal lengths. It is even smaller and lighter than the 35-135mm, making it a favorite among Canon users. It has 15 elements in 12 groups, an angle of view of 75° to 23°20′, a filter size of 58mm, and a minimum focusing distance of 19 inches (50 cm); it is 2.8 inches (7.2 cm) long, and weighs 13.1 ounces (375 g).

Canon EF 28-135mm f/3.5-5.6 IS USM: This lens quickly became a favorite of mine (Bob Shell) for its very useful focal length range and the implementation of IS technology, which frees me from a tripod or monopod when working outdoors in almost any light. I consider this just about the ideal lens for the great majority of my photography work, both in the studio and outdoors. While it is not an L-series lens and therefore not as highly corrected as the 28-80mm L that I used for so many years, the gain of IS technology more than makes up for any slight loss in image quality, and the number of blurred images I get due to camera motion is minuscule. The lens uses 16 elements in 12 groups, with one glass molded aspheric element. The lens focuses as close as 19.7 inches (50 cm), close enough for most applications other than true macro. The lens accepts 72mm filters and measures 3.8 x 3.1 inches (9.68 x 7.84 cm); its weight is 17.6 ounces (500 g).

Telephoto Zoom Lenses

Until recently, heated debates among proponents and opponents of zoom lenses still raged. Numerous quality improvements on lenses with variable focal lengths have reduced the problem to the question of maximum aperture (speed) versus convenience. Fixed focal lengths will always be available to solve special problems, but a user-friendly zoom lens is quite welcome even in professional circles. The advantage of framing a subject in an ideal manner without changing camera position is tempting. Many photographers, however, forget that the relationship between foreground and background changes dramatically when you consider a distance of 60 feet (20 m) at a focal length of 200mm or a distance of 24 feet (8 m) at a focal length of 80mm. This is not obvious based on the main subject, but based instead on the size and sharpness of objects at different distances in the background.

Many photographers, as well, think and see in focal lengths; they have a 50mm, 100mm, and 200mm view stored in their heads. They know from the very beginning how the picture will look and how to represent the foreground relative to the background. A zoom lens makes this learning process more difficult, but it opens up creative possibilities, such as the so-called zoom effect, a radial blur.

The decision of what lens to buy depends on different requirements. The easiest criterion would be to focus on the Luxury (L) series. A professional certainly will look at the L lenses with careful consideration, whereas an amateur photographer will probably make a decision based more on his or her budget. Canon's 35-350mm L super zoom is certainly interesting to those who want to get along with the smallest number of lenses.

A decision on the focal length range is more difficult. Because it is convenient, the focal length range from 80mm to 200mm has become the most popular. By going with an 80-200mm f/4.5-5.6 II and a wide-angle zoom lens, such as the 28-80mm f/3.5-5.6, the entire range from 28mm to 200mm can be covered with just two lenses.

The close-up range of the 80-200mm lens set at 200mm at 4.9 feet (1.5 m) allows the capture of a butterfly at a convincing size because at 200mm the size of the subject area is 5.2 x 7.9 inches

(13.3 x 20 cm). A special macro setting and a distance of 3.6 feet (1.2 m) provides a subject area that at 200mm is not much bigger than a postcard, and at 50mm is still approximately 16 x 24 inches (40 x 60 cm). And remember, a wide aperture should not be used with a macro setting. A reduction by at least two f/stops from wide open is recommended. The type of macro setting on telephoto zoom lenses is a technical by-product of the lens design and can also be used in AF mode.

Most of Canon's telezoom lenses are of reasonable weight, ranging from the 8.8 ounces (250 g) of the 80-200mm f/4.5-5.6 II to the 1.5 pounds (695 g) of the 100-300mm f/5.6L. Only the 35-350mm f/3.5-5.6L USM and 70-200mm f/2.8L USM are heavier, weighing 3 pounds (1.385 g) and 2.7 pounds (1.275 g) respectively.

The telezooms are convenient to carry and easy to handle. The only disadvantage is their relatively small maximum aperture, based on the viewpoint of photographers who like to emphasize the particularly photogenic boundaries of light. Considering a focal length of 35mm, the f/3.5 maximum lens aperture is not exactly overwhelming, and considering a focal length of 350mm, an f/5.6 maximum lens aperture is barely adequate; an exception is the Canon zoom EF 70-200mm f/2.8L USM. Those who have a normal lens (like the 50mm f/1.8 II) and want to stay at a reasonable cost should consider either the 75-300mm f/4.0-5.6 II or the 75-300mm f/4.0-5.6 II USM.

A photographer who is not afraid to set up a tripod once in a while and has the time and patience will find the EF 100-300mm f/4.5-5.6 USM an ideal lens. Even the close-up setting of 4.9 feet (1.5 m) with a six-times-larger scale of reproduction is convincing compared with a normal lens. The L version of the 100-300 features an overall upgrade in quality with an additional UD lens and apochromatic correction. The 70-200mm and both 100-300mm zoom lenses have a so-called macro setting, which has only minimal differences in the scale of reproduction. With the shortest focal length setting, the subject is somewhat larger than a piece of letter-size paper; with the longest setting, it is somewhat smaller.

Canon EF 35-350mm f/3.5-5.6L USM: This super-zoom lens, which covers the largest focal length range of all the Canon zoom lenses, ranges from wide angle all the way to super telephoto.

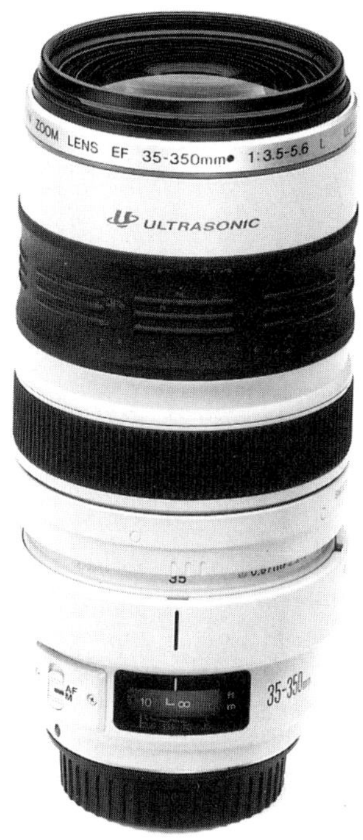

Canon EF 35-350mm f/3.5-5.6L USM

This was achieved by a separate adjustment microprocessor in the lens and a multiple group design comprised of five lens groups, all of which move when the focal length is changed. The movements of each group, however, are very short because each lens group exhibits an optimal index of refraction. Focusing takes place through a rear component focusing system, run smoothly and rapidly by an ultrasonic motor, that allows sharp focusing in the wide-angle range down to 24 inches (60 cm). In the greater telephoto range, the close-up limit is 6.6 feet (2.2 m). This allows the smallest imaging field of 6.1 x 9.7 inches (15.5 x 24.7 cm).

Two UD glass elements reduce chromatic aberration and ensure sharp reproduction over the entire range. The lens, which is surprisingly compact, has a length of less than 7 inches (17 cm), weighs 3 pounds (1.385 kg), and can even be used for hand-held shots if supported with a rifle stock or hand grip.

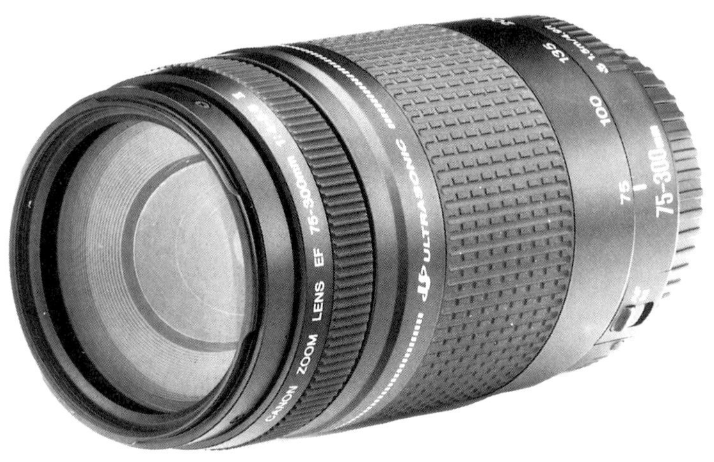

Canon EF 75-300mm f/4.0-5.6II USM

Canon EF 75-300mm f/4.0-5.6 II USM: This zoom lens allows an inexpensive beginning into the telephoto realm. Its low weight is 17.3 ounces (495 g), 30% lighter than the EF 100-300mm f/5.6L. At a length of 4.8 inches (12 cm), it can be used quite comfortably for handheld shots. The optical system consists of 13 elements in nine groups; the shortest focusing distance is 4.9 feet (1.5 m). It also comes in a slightly lighter weight DC Micro Motor model.

Canon EF 75-300mm f/4.0-5.6 IS USM: With this lens, Canon has made the world's first SLR interchangeable lens with Image

Canon EF 75-300mm f/4.0-5.6 IS USM

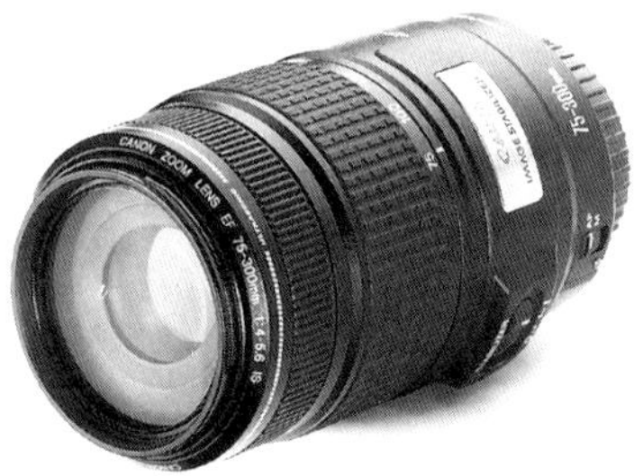

Canon EF 100-300mm f/4.5-5.6 USM

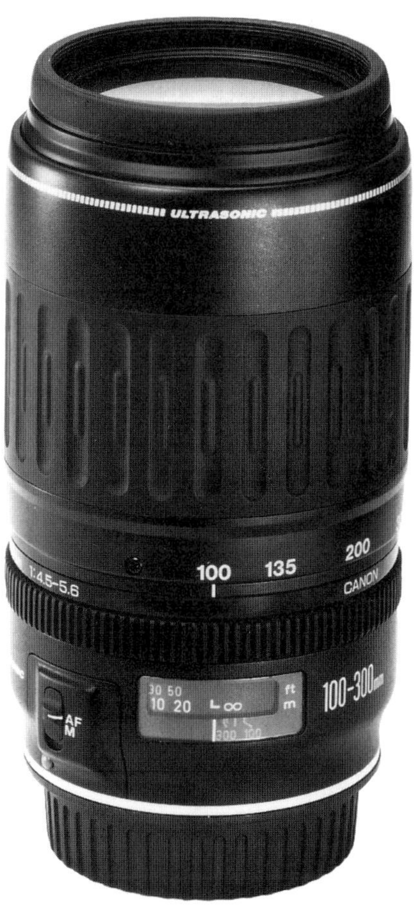

Stabilization (IS). This combination of optical and electronic technology compensates for camera and lens movement, allowing you to shoot handheld at slower shutter speeds (up to two stops!). The lens has 15 elements in 10 groups, a minimum focusing distance of 4.9 feet (1.5 m), and a filter size of 58mm. This lens is 5.4 inches (13.7 cm) long and weighs 23.5 ounces (670 g).

Canon EF 100-300mm f/4.5-5.6 USM: This is a very compact lens offering exceptionally fast autofocusing due to its optical system, which has only three inner moving elements. The complete optical construction consists of 13 elements in 10 groups. The size of the lens is 4.75 inches (12.1 cm) long, with a maximum diameter of 2.9 inches (7.3 cm). The weight is 19 ounces (540 g), and the angle of view covered by this zoom lens is 24° to 8°15´.

Canon EF 100-400mm f/4.5-5.6 ISL USM: This new Canon EF lens offers the extremely versatile range of 100-400mm, an ideal range for sports, wildlife, and many other types of telephoto photography. The lens speed of f/4.6-5.6 may not seem all that fast, but this is more than made up for by the use of IS technology, which permits this lens to be used handheld even at slow shutter speeds. Because it is from Canon's L series, this is a fully professional lens of the highest optical quality. The optical formula consists of 17 elements in 14 groups and includes one each of fluorite and Super UD glass. Filter size is 77 mm. The lens measures 7.4 x 3.6 inches (1.89 x 9.2 cm) and weighs 3 pounds (1.385 kg).

Canon Extenders EF 1.4x and EF 2x

Extenders are optical accessories that are placed between the camera and the lens to extend the effective focal length of the main lens. The numbers 1.4x and 2x indicate the factor by which the lens' focal length is increased. This focal length extension produces a reduction of speed (or effective aperture). In the case of the EF 1.4x extender, this is one stop, and in the case of the EF 2x extender, two stops. All functions governing aperture and AF control are maintained. If the aperture of the lens attached to the converter is less than f/5.6, however, the AF system won't function properly, and the lens must be focused manually.

Although some aftermarket extenders or teleconverters have inexpensive, low-quality optics, Canon converters are high-quality lens systems specifically designed for use with Canon telephoto lenses. They can be expensive, but they add tremendous versatility to a lens outfit.

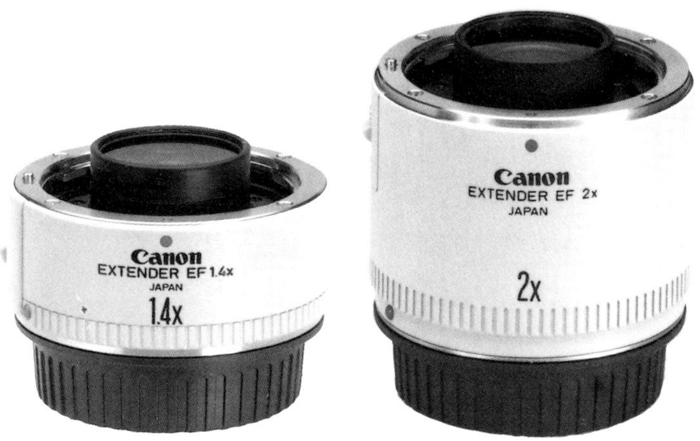

Canon makes two EF extenders, the 1.4x and the 2x.

Macro Lenses

Canon EF 50mm f/2.5 Compact Macro: Macro lenses are designed for flat-field reproduction and high performance in the close-distance range. The 50mm macro features particularly high resolution, excellent contrast, and optimal image-area flatness. The minimum focusing distance is 9.1 inches (23 cm); at this point, a subject is recorded at half its original size (a 1:2 reproduction ratio) on the film.

When pictures are taken of flowers, insects, or other small subjects in nature, Aperture-Priority (Av) mode comes in handy. Using this feature, however, will not eliminate the problem of shallow depth of field (which is barely 6 mm at f/11 and a scale of reproduction of 1:2). This effect is inherent in close-up photography, but with proper technique, it can be reduced to an acceptable degree. For example, flowers can be framed so that the largest part of the blossom is parallel to the film plane, making depth of field not a critical factor in the final photo. The same applies when photographing a subject such as a beetle. It is best photographed directly from the top or the side, so that the largest area of its body is parallel to the film plane. With all close-up work, use of a tripod is recommended.

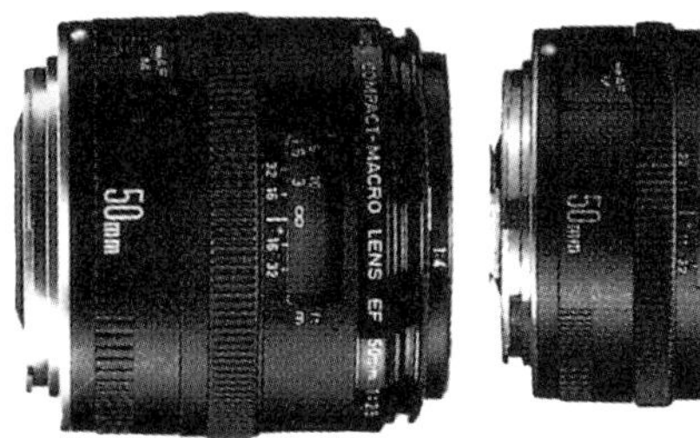

A 50mm comparison: The EF 50mm f/1.8 (left) vs. the EF 50mm f/2.5 compact micro.

Canon offers the EF Life Size Converter as an accessory for use with this lens. This converter, which is mounted between camera body and lens, permits shots at a scale of reproduction between 1:4 and 1:1 and compensates for the spherical aberration in the close-up and macro ranges.

The EF 50mm f/2.5 compact macro is also suitable as a universal lens in all shooting ranges. The AFD motor allows automatic focusing from infinity to a scale of 1:0.5 in only 1.5 seconds. Manual focusing is also possible. The lens is 2.5 inches (6.3 cm) long and weighs 9.9 ounces (280 g).

Canon EF 100mm f/2.8 Macro: This fast telephoto lens was designed specifically for macro shots up to a scale of 1:1 without additional intermediate rings or the EF Life Size Converter. A focus-limiting switch permits selection between two distance ranges; one is within the macro range of 12.4 inches (31.5 cm) and 22.8 inches (57.9 cm), and the other goes from 22.8 inches (57.9 cm) to infinity. The AF DC Micro Motor covers this distance in exactly one second. The smallest subject area is 0.5 x 1.4 inches (1.3 x 3.6 cm). A system of 10 elements in nine groups provides a viewing angle of 24°. The lens has a length of 4.1 inches (10.5 cm) and a weight of 22 ounces (650 g).

Canon EF 180mm f/3.5L Macro: This lens offers all of the conveniences of the EF 100mm f/2.8 macro but with a longer focal length for those who need more working distance between lens and subject or a different perspective.

Tilt-Shift Lenses

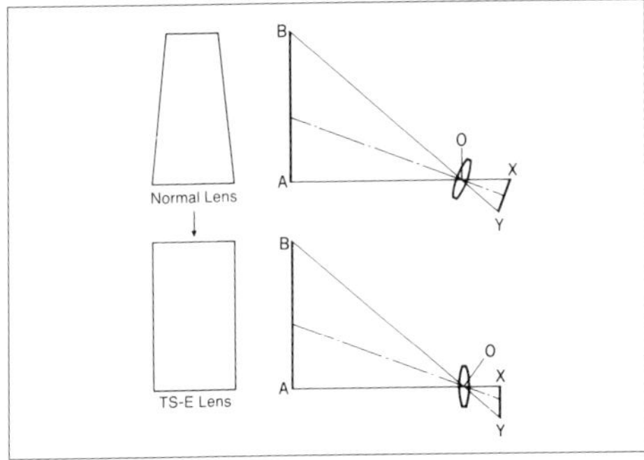

This simple diagram illustrates how a tilt-shift (TS-E) lens eliminates the need to tilt the camera upward when photographing a building, thus eliminating perspective distortion.

Tilt-shift lenses allow the correction of the notorious converging verticals or distorted parallel lines that form when the film plane and the subject plane are not parallel. This is the case whenever, for example, large buildings are shot and the camera must be tilted upward to capture the entire view. Without this lens, tilting the foreground becomes disproportionately dominant, and only part of the building is in the picture. By shifting a lens out of the optical axis, this view can be adjusted in the desired direction. Rather than simply making perspective control lenses, as other makers have done, Canon has combined this perspective control shift with tilt capability, calling them tilt-shift (TS-E) lenses.

These special Canon EOS lenses come in three focal lengths: TS-E 24mm f/3.5 L, TS-E 45mm f/2.8, and TS-E 90mm f/2.8. All three lenses exhibit excellent image quality and ensure maximum contrast, resolving power, and brilliance of color rendition. The TS-E 24mm f/3.5L lens is equipped with a ground and polished aspherical element, which assures this lens' optical performance is at the same level as the other TS-E lenses, despite its shorter focal length.

All three lenses can be tilted by +/–8°, and the entire optical system can be shifted by +/–11 mm; 4 mm of this scale is marked in red only on the super-wide-angle lens. When tilting is combined with maximum shift, vignetting may occur in this red range.

Canon TS-E 90mm f/2.8 Tilt-Shift Lens

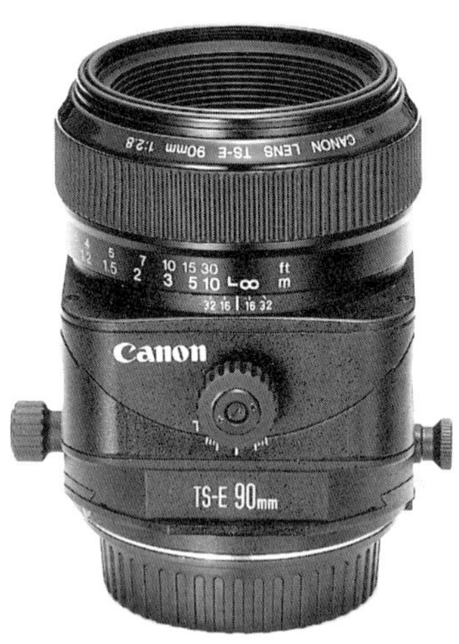

Custom Functions

The Canon EOS-3 offers 18 Custom Functions (numbered 0-17), which allow you to override the camera's factory (default) programming, and set the camera for your personal needs or preferences. Each Custom Function has two or more variables; the factory default is designated by a zero (0) on all.

You can access a Custom Function by pressing the CF button under the panel door on the camera, and using the Main Dial to scroll through the CF numbers. For example, suppose you want to use Custom Function 2 to have the film leader protrude from the cassette. Press the CF button and turn the Main Dial until "F2" appears on the LCD panel. Press the CF button again to change the setting from the factory default ("0") to the setting you want ("1"). Press lightly on the shutter release button to lock in the changed setting. Then, each time you rewind the film, the leader will be left protruding from the cassette.

To revert to the original setting, repeat the procedure and change the setting from 1 back to 0. You can return all the settings to their factory defaults by pressing the CF button and then pressing the CLEAR button below it.

This section lists and describes the Custom Functions; in addition, many of them are explained throughout the text of this guide. Note also that Canon provides with the EOS-3 a handy wallet card listing the Custom Functions.

CF no.	Function	Setting	Description
0	Focusing screen characteristics	0	Sets compensation data for new laser matte screen (Ec-N, Ec-R)
		1	Sets compensation data for laser matte screen (Ec-A, B, C, CII, D, H, I, L)
1	Auto film rewind mode	0	Automatic high-speed rewind
		1	Manually activated high-speed rewind
		2	Automatic quiet rewind
		3	Manually activated quiet rewind
2	Film leader position	0	Rewind film leader into the cartridge
		1	Leave film leader outside the cartridge
3	Film speed setting method	0	Set automatically by DX code
		1	Set manually
4	AF activation	0	Enables AF operation by pressing the shutter button halfway; enables AE lock with the AE lock button
		1	Enables AF operation by pressing the AE lock button; enables AE lock by pressing the shutter button halfway
		2	Enables AF operation by pressing the shutter button halfway; enables AE lock with the AE lock button
		3	Enables AF operation by pressing the AE lock button; enables AF operation by pressing the shutter button halfway
5	Manual shutter speed/aperture (Tv/Av) settings	0	In Manual mode, the shutter speed is selected with the Main Dial, and the aperture is selected

			by turning the Quick Control Dial or by pressing the exposure compensation button (+/–) and turning the Main Dial
		1	In Manual mode, the shutter speed is selected with the Quick Control Dial or by pressing the +/– button and turning the Main Dial, and the aperture is set with the Main Dial
		2	Option 0 set for both Tv and Av; aperture settable without lens attached to camera
		3	Option 1 set for both Tv and Av; aperture settable without lens attached to camera
6	Increments for Tv, Av, exposure compensation, flash exposure compensation, and AEB (1/3, 1/2, or whole stops)	0	Shutter speed, aperture, exposure compensation, flash exposure compensation, and autoexposure bracketing (AEB) values are set in 1/3-stop increments
		1	Shutter speed and aperture values are adjusted in full stops; exposure compensation, flash exposure compensation, and AEB values are set in 1/3-stop increments
		2	Shutter speed, aperture, exposure compensation, flash exposure compensation, and AEB values are adjusted in 1/2-stop increments
7	USM lens with electronic ring manual focus (50mm f/1.0L, 85mm f/1.2L, 200mm f/1.8L, 300mm 2.8L, 400mm f/2.8L II, 500mm 4.5L, 600mm f/4.0L, 1200mm f/5.6L)	0	Enables electronic-ring manual focusing after One Shot AF or AF failure (CF-4-1, 4-3 enable manual focus even before focus is achieved)
		1	Disables electronic-ring manual focusing after One Shot AF or AF failure (CF-4-1, 4-3 enable manual focus before focus is achieved)

CF no.	Function	Setting	Description
		2	Disables electronic-ring manual focusing after One Shot AF or AF failure (manual focus disabled in all cases)
8	Frame counter	0	Count up (countdown during rewind)
		1	Count down (countdown during rewind)
9	Autoexposure sequence (bracketing) and auto cancellation	0	Takes three shots—underexposed, correct (metered), and overexposed
		1	Takes three shots—underexposed, correct, and overexposed (not canceled during L, lens change, film loading, and rewind)
		2	Takes three shots—correct, underexposed, and overexposed
		3	Takes three shots—correct, underexposed, and overexposed (not canceled during L, lens change, film loading, and rewind)
			Note: Options 0 and 2 cancel when any of the following occurs: CLEAR, Speedlite recharges, Bulb mode, main switch to L, lens changed, film loaded, autoloading, or rewind; options 1 and 3 cancel when any of the following occurs: CLEAR, Speedlite recharges, Bulb mode
10	Active AF area illumination	0	Always illuminated: (1) During eye control—The focusing point flashes brightly when the shutter button is pressed halfway, when the focusing point is eye selected, and when focus is achieved. If the shutter button is still pressed halfway after focus is achieved, the focusing point keeps flashing

			dimly while the lens operates (2) During manual selection—The focusing point flashes brightly when the shutter button is pressed halfway and when focus is achieved. If the shutter button is still pressed halfway after focus is achieved, the focusing point keeps flashing dimly while the lens operates (3) During automatic selection—The focusing point that achieves focus flashes brightly
		1	Never illuminated
		2	Lights only when the condition changes
		3	Increases brightness level
11	Focusing point selection method	0	Focusing point selected by pressing the focusing point selector and rotating the Main or Quick Control Dial
		1	Focusing point selected by pressing the exposure compensation button (+/–) and rotating the Main or Quick Control Dial (reverses the function of the focusing point selector and the +/– button)
		2	Focusing point selected by pressing the +/– button and rotating the Main or Quick Control Dial. (Pressing the focusing point selector while the shutter button is pressed halfway switches from manual to automatic focusing point selection.)
		3	Focusing point selected by pressing the FEL button and rotating the Main or Quick Control Dial (reverses the functions of the focusing point selector and the FEL button)

CF no.	Function	Setting	Description
12	Mirror lockup (mirror prerelease)	0	The reflex mirror flips up immediately prior to exposure
		1	The reflex mirror flips up when the shutter button is pressed; exposure is initiated by pressing the shutter button a second time. Mirror lockup is effective for 30 seconds
13	Focusing point and spot metering	0	Eye control with 45 focusing points; user-selected focusing-point-linked spot metering
		1	Eye control with 11 focusing points; user-selected focusing-point-linked spot metering (limits the number of focusing points selectable manually or by eye to 11, and enables spot metering linked to focusing points)
		2	Eye control with 11 focusing points; user-selected center-spot metering (limits the number of focusing points selectable manually or by eye to 11, and restricts spot metering to central area)
14	Automatic flash control	0	Enabled automatic reduction of TTL autoflash output levels
		1	Disabled automatic reduction of TTL autoflash output level. Recommended for heavy backlight or whenever flash compensation is set by photographer, effective with E-TTL, A-TTL, and TTL flash exposure control
15	Flash sync timing (effective only with EX-Series *Speedlites* not equipped with a flash sync switch)	0	Front-curtain synchronization
		1	Rear-curtain synchronization

16	Safety switch for Tv and Av autoexposure	0	Disabled
		1	Enabled (allows camera to override photographer-set Tv or Av values to achieve correct exposure in marginal lighting conditions)
17	Expansion of AF area	0	Standard (single point)
		1	Manually selected focusing point area expands by one point horizontally and vertically. (Autofocusing is first attempted with the center focusing point. If the center focusing point cannot achieve focus, one of the adjacent focusing points is used to achieve focus. This is an effective backup for achieving focus during predictive autofocus.)
		2	The camera expands the focusing point selection area by one point vertically and two points horizontally. (The camera automatically sets the range of focusing points to be used to suit the lens focal length and predictive autofocus. This is an effective backup for achieving focus when a super telephoto lens is used.)

Custom Functions 4 and 7 Combinations

	CF 4-0	**CF 4-1**	**CF 4-2**	**CF 4-3**
CF 7-0	X/O	O/O	X/O	O/O
CF 7-1	X/X	O/X	X/X	O/X
CF 7-2	X/X	X/X	X/X	X/X

O = Electronic ring and manual focus possible before and after autofocus is achieved. (Applies only to EF lenses with electron metering manual focus; see CF 7 listing in chart.)

X = Disabled.